JAMESTOWN  EDUCAT

G000162497

Timed Readings
in Social Studies

BOOK 3

**25 Two-Part Lessons with Questions for
Building Reading Speed and Comprehension**

 **Glencoe**

New York, New York   Columbus, Ohio   Chicago, Illinois   Peoria, Illinois   Woodland Hills, California

JAMESTOWN  EDUCATION

Mc Graw Hill **Glencoe**

The **McGraw·Hill** Companies

ISBN: 0-07-845801-3

Copyright © 2004 The McGraw-Hill Companies, Inc. All rights reserved. Except as permitted under the United States Copyright Act, no part of this publication may be reproduced or distributed in any form or by any means, or stored in a database or retrieval system, without prior written permission of the publisher.

Send all queries to:
Glencoe/McGraw-Hill
8787 Orion Place
Columbus, OH 43240-4027

4 5 6 7 8 9 10 021 08 07 06 05

CONTENTS

TO THE STUDENT

You probably talk at an average rate of about 150 words a minute. If you are a reader of average ability, you read at a rate of about 250 words a minute. So your reading speed is nearly twice as fast as your speaking or listening speed. This example shows that reading is one of the fastest ways to get information.

The purpose of this book is to help you increase your reading rate and understand what you read. The 25 lessons in this book will also give you practice in reading social studies articles and in preparing for tests in which you must read and understand nonfiction passages within a certain time limit.

Reading Faster and Better

Following are some strategies that you can use to read the articles in each lesson.

Previewing

Previewing before you read is a very important step. This helps you to get an idea of what a selection is about and to recall any previous knowledge you have about the subject. Here are the steps to follow when previewing.

Read the title. Titles are designed not only to announce the subject but also to make the reader think. Ask yourself questions such as What can I learn from the title? What thoughts does it bring to mind?

What do I already know about this subject?

Read the first sentence. If they are short, read the first two sentences. The opening sentence is the writer's opportunity to get your attention. Some writers announce what they hope to tell you in the selection. Some writers state their purpose for writing; others just try to get your attention.

Read the last sentence. If it is short, read the final two sentences. The closing sentence is the writer's last chance to get ideas across to you. Some writers repeat the main idea once more. Some writers draw a conclusion—this is what they have been leading up to. Other writers summarize their thoughts; they tie all the facts together.

Skim the entire selection. Glance through the selection quickly to see what other information you can pick up. Look for anything that will help you read fluently and with understanding. Are there names, dates, or numbers? If so, you may have to read more slowly.

Reading for Meaning

Here are some ways to make sure you are making sense of what you read.

Build your concentration. You cannot understand what you read if you are not concentrating. When you discover that your thoughts are straying, correct the situation right away. Avoid distractions and distracting situations. Keep in mind the information you learned from previewing. This will help focus your attention on the selection.

Read in thought groups. Try to see meaningful combinations of words—phrases, clauses, or sentences. If you look at only one word at a time (called word-by-word reading), both your comprehension and your reading speed suffer.

Ask yourself questions. To sustain the pace you have set for yourself and to maintain a high level of concentration and comprehension, ask yourself questions such as What does this mean? or How can I use this information? as you read.

Finding the Main Ideas

The paragraph is the basic unit of meaning. If you can quickly discover and understand the main idea of each paragraph, you will build your comprehension of the selection.

Find the topic sentence. The topic sentence, which contains the main idea, often is the first sentence of a paragraph. It is followed by sentences that support, develop, or explain the main idea. Sometimes a topic sentence comes at the end of a paragraph. When it does, the supporting details come first, building the base for the topic sentence. Some paragraphs do not have a topic sentence; all of the sentences combine to create a meaningful idea.

Understand paragraph structure. Every well-written paragraph has a purpose. The purpose may be to inform, define, explain, or illustrate. The purpose should always relate to the main idea and expand on it. As you read each paragraph, see how the body of the paragraph tells you more about the main idea.

Relate ideas as you read. As you read the selection, notice how the writer puts together ideas. As you discover the relationship between the ideas, the main ideas come through quickly and clearly.

Mastering Reading Comprehension

Reading fast is not useful if you don't remember or understand what you read. The two exercises in Part A provide a check on how well you have understood the article.

Recalling Facts

These multiple-choice questions provide a quick check to see how well you recall important information from the article. As you learn to apply the reading strategies described earlier, you should be able to answer these questions more successfully.

Understanding Ideas

These questions require you to think about the main ideas in the article. Some main ideas are stated in the article; others are not. To answer some of the questions, you need to draw conclusions about what you read.

The five exercises in Part B require multiple answers. These exercises provide practice in applying comprehension and critical thinking skills that you can use in all your reading.

Recognizing Words in Context

Always check to see whether the words around an unfamiliar word—its context—can give you a clue to the word's meaning. A word generally appears in a context related to its meaning.

Suppose, for example, that you are unsure of the meaning of the word *expired* in the following passage:

> Vera wanted to check out a book, but her library card had expired. She had to borrow my card, because she didn't have time to renew hers.

You could begin to figure out the meaning of *expired* by asking yourself a question such as, What could have happened to Vera's library card that would make her need to borrow someone else's card? You might realize that if Vera had to renew her card, its usefulness must have come to an end or run out. This would lead you to conclude that the word *expired* must mean "to come to an end" or "to run out." You would be right. The context suggested the meaning.

Context can also affect the meaning of a word you already know. The word *key,* for instance, has many meanings. There are musical keys, door keys, and keys to solving a mystery. The context in which the word *key* occurs will tell you which meaning is correct.

Sometimes a word is explained by the words that immediately follow it. The subject of a sentence and your knowledge about that subject might also help you determine the meaning of an unknown word. Try to decide the meaning of the word *revive* in the following sentence:

> Sunshine and water will revive those drooping plants.

The compound subject is *sunshine* and *water.* You know that plants need light and water to survive and that drooping plants are not healthy. You can figure out that *revive* means "to bring back to health."

Distinguishing Fact from Opinion

Every day you are called upon to sort out fact and opinion. Because much of what you read and hear contains both facts and opinions, you need to be able to tell the two apart.

Facts are statements that can be proved. The proof must be objective and verifiable. You must be able to check for yourself to confirm a fact.

Look at the following facts. Notice that they can be checked for accuracy and confirmed. Suggested sources for verification appear in parentheses.

- Abraham Lincoln was the 16th president of the United States. (Consult biographies, social studies books, encyclopedias, and similar sources.)

- Earth revolves around the Sun. (Research in encyclopedias or astronomy books; ask knowledgeable people.)

- Dogs walk on four legs. (See for yourself.)

Opinions are statements that cannot be proved. There is no objective evidence you can consult to check the truthfulness of an opinion. Unlike facts, opinions express personal beliefs or judgments. Opinions reveal how someone feels about a subject, not the facts about that subject. You might agree or disagree with someone's opinion, but you cannot prove it right or wrong.

Look at the following opinions. The reasons these statements are classified as opinions appear in parentheses.

- Abraham Lincoln was born to be a president. (You cannot prove this by referring to birth records. There is no evidence to support this belief.)

- Earth is the only planet in our solar system where intelligent life exists. (There is no proof of this. It may be proved true some day, but for now it is just an educated guess—not a fact.)

- The dog is a human's best friend. (This is not a fact; your best friend might not be a dog.)

As you read, be aware that facts and opinions are often mixed together. Both are useful to you as a reader. But to evaluate what you read and to read intelligently, you need to know the difference between the two.

Keeping Events in Order

Sequence, or chronological order, is the order of events in a story or article or the order of steps in a process. Paying attention to the sequence of events or steps will help you follow what is happening, predict what might happen next, and make sense of a passage.

To make the sequence as clear as possible, writers often use signal words to help the reader get a more exact idea of when things happen. Following is a list of frequently used signal words and phrases:

until	first
next	then
before	after
finally	later
when	while
during	now
at the end	by the time
as soon as	in the beginning

Signal words and phrases are also useful when a writer chooses to relate details or events out of sequence. You need to pay careful attention to determine the correct chronological order.

Making Correct Inferences

Much of what you read *suggests* more than it *says*. Writers often do not state ideas directly in a text. They can't. Think of the time and space it would take to state every idea. And think of how boring that would be! Instead, writers leave it to you, the reader, to fill in the information they leave out—to make inferences. You do this by combining clues in the story or article with knowledge from your own experience.

You make many inferences every day. Suppose, for example, that you are visiting a friend's house for the first time. You see a bag of kitty litter. You infer (make an inference) that the family has a cat. Another day you overhear a conversation. You catch the names of two actors and the words *scene, dialogue,* and *directing.* You infer that the people are discussing a movie or play.

In these situations and others like them, you infer unstated information from what you observe or read. Readers must make inferences in order to understand text.

Be careful about the inferences you make. One set of facts may suggest several inferences. Some of these inferences could be faulty. A correct inference must be supported by evidence.

Remember that bag of kitty litter that caused you to infer that your friend has a cat? That could be a faulty inference. Perhaps your friend's family uses the kitty litter on their icy sidewalks to create traction. To be sure your inference is correct, you need more evidence.

Understanding Main Ideas

The main idea is the most important idea in a paragraph or passage—the idea that provides purpose and direction. The rest of the selection explains, develops, or supports the main idea. Without a main idea, there would be only a collection of unconnected thoughts.

In the following paragraph, the main idea is printed in italics. As you read, observe how the other sentences develop or explain the main idea.

Typhoon Chris hit with full fury today on the central coast of Japan. Heavy rain from the storm flooded the area. High waves carried many homes into the sea. People now fear that the heavy rains will cause mudslides in the central part of the country. The number of people killed by the storm may climb past the 200 mark by Saturday.

In this paragraph, the main-idea statement appears first. It is followed by sentences that explain, support, or give details. Sometimes the main idea appears at the end of a paragraph. Writers often put the main idea at the end of a paragraph when their purpose is to persuade or convince. Readers may be more open to a new idea if the reasons for it are presented first.

As you read the following paragraph, think about the overall impact of the supporting ideas. Their purpose is to convince the reader that the main idea in the last sentence should be accepted.

Last week there was a head-on collision at Huntington and Canton streets. Just a month ago a pedestrian was struck there. Fortunately, she was only slightly injured. In the past year, there have been more accidents there than at any other corner in the city. In fact, nearly 10 percent of all accidents in the city occur at the corner. This intersection is very dangerous, and a traffic signal should be installed there before a life is lost.

The details in the paragraph progress from least important to most important. They achieve their full effect in the main idea statement at the end.

In many cases, the main idea is not expressed in a single sentence. The reader is called upon to interpret all of the ideas expressed in the paragraph and to decide upon a main idea. Read the following paragraph.

> The American author Jack London was once a pupil at the Cole Grammar School in Oakland, California. Each morning the class sang a song. When the teacher noticed that Jack wouldn't sing, she sent him to the principal. He returned to class with a note. The note said that Jack could be excused from singing with the class if he would write an essay every morning.

In this paragraph, the reader has to interpret the individual ideas and to decide on a main idea. This main idea seems reasonable: Jack London's career as a writer began with a punishment in grammar school.

Understanding the concept of the main idea and knowing how to find it is important. Transferring that understanding to your reading and study is also important.

Working Through a Lesson

Part A

1. **Preview the article.** Locate the timed selection in Part A of the lesson that you are going to read. Wait for your teacher's signal to preview. You will have 20 seconds for previewing. Follow the previewing steps described on page 2.

2. **Read the article.** When your teacher gives you the signal, begin reading. Read carefully so that you will be able to answer questions about what you have read. When you finish reading, look at the board and note your reading time. Write this time at the bottom of the page on the line labeled Reading Time.

3. **Complete the exercises.** Answer the 10 questions that follow the article. There are 5 fact questions and 5 idea questions. Choose the best answer to each question and put an X in that box.

4. **Correct your work.** Use the Answer Key at the back of the book to check your answers. Circle any wrong answer and put an X in the box you should have marked. Record the number of correct answers on the appropriate line at the end of the lesson.

Part B

1. **Preview and read the passage.** Use the same techniques you

used to read Part A. Think about what you are reading.

2. **Complete the exercises.** Instructions are given for answering each category of question. There are 15 responses for you to record.

3. **Correct your work.** Use the Answer Key at the back of the book. Circle any wrong answer and write the correct letter or number next to it. Record the number of correct answers on the appropriate line at the end of the lesson.

Plotting Your Progress

1. **Find your reading rate.** Turn to the Reading Rate graph on page 116. Put an X at the point where the vertical line that represents the lesson intersects your reading time, shown along the left-hand side. The right-hand side of the graph will reveal your words-per-minute reading speed.

2. **Find your comprehension score.** Add your scores for Part A and Part B to determine your total number of correct answers. Turn to the Comprehension Score Graph on page 117. Put an X at the point where the vertical line that represents your lesson intersects your total correct answers, shown along the left-hand side. The right-hand side of the graph will show the percentage of questions you answered correctly.

3. **Complete the Comprehension Skills Profile.** Turn to page 118. Record your incorrect answers for the Part B exercises. The five Part B skills are listed along the bottom. There are five columns of boxes, one column for each question. For every incorrect answer, put an X in a box for that skill.

To get the most benefit from these lessons, you need to take charge of your own progress in improving your reading speed and comprehension. Studying these graphs will help you to see whether your reading rate is increasing and to determine what skills you need to work on. Your teacher will also review the graphs to check your progress.

TO THE TEACHER

About the Series

Timed Readings Plus in Social Studies includes 10 books at reading levels 4–13, with one book at each level. Book One contains material at a fourth-grade reading level; Book Two at a fifth-grade level, and so on. The readability level is determined by the Fry Readability Scale and is not to be confused with grade or age level of the student. The books are designed for use with students at middle school level and above.

The purposes of the series are as follows:

- to provide systematic, structured reading practice that helps students improve their reading rate and comprehension skills

- to give students practice in reading and understanding informational articles in the content area of social studies

- to give students experience in reading various text types—informational, expository, narrative, and prescriptive

- to prepare students for taking standardized tests that include timed reading passages in various content areas

- to provide materials with a wide range of reading levels so that students can continue to practice and improve their reading rate and comprehension skills

Because the books are designed for use with students at designated reading levels rather than in a particular grade, the social studies topics in this series are not correlated to any grade-level curriculum. Most standardized tests require students to read and comprehend social studies passages. This series provides an opportunity for students to become familiar with the particular requirements of reading social studies. For example, the vocabulary in a social studies article is important. Students need to know certain words in order to understand the concepts and the information.

Each book in the series contains 25 two-part lessons. Part A focuses on improving reading rate. This section of the lesson consists of a 400-word timed informational article on a social studies topic followed by two multiple-choice exercises. Recalling Facts includes five fact questions; Understanding Ideas includes five critical thinking questions.

Part B concentrates on building mastery in critical areas of comprehension. This section consists of a nontimed passage—the "plus" passage—followed by five exercises that address five major comprehension skills. The passage varies in length; its subject matter relates to the content of the timed selection.

Timed Reading and Comprehension

Timed reading is the best-known method of improving reading speed. There is no point in someone's reading at an accelerated speed if the person does not understand what she or he is reading. Nothing is more important than comprehension in reading. The main purpose of reading is to gain knowledge and insight, to understand the information that the writer and the text are communicating.

Few students will be able to read a passage once and answer all of the questions correctly. A score of 70 or 80 percent correct is normal. If the student gets 90 or 100 percent correct, he or she is either reading too slowly or the material is at too low a reading level. A comprehension or critical thinking score of less than 70 percent indicates a need for improvement.

One method of improving comprehension and critical thinking skills is for the student to go back and study each incorrect answer. First, the student should reread the question carefully. It is surprising how many students get the wrong answer simply because they have not read the question carefully. Then the student should look back in the passage to find the place where the question is answered, reread that part of the passage, and think about how to arrive at the correct answer. It is important to be able to recognize a correct answer when it is embedded in the text. Teacher guidance or class discussion will help the student find an answer.

Speed Versus Comprehension

It is not unusual for comprehension scores to decline as reading rate increases during the early weeks of timed readings. If this happens, students should attempt to level off their speed—but not lower it—and concentrate more on comprehension. Usually, if students maintain the higher speed and concentrate on comprehension, scores will gradually improve and within a week or two be back up to normal levels of 70 to 80 percent.

It is important to achieve a proper balance between speed and comprehension. An inefficient reader typically reads everything at one speed, usually slowly. Some poor readers, however, read rapidly but without satisfactory comprehension. It is important to achieve a balance between speed and comprehension. The practice that this series provides enables students to increase their reading speed while maintaining normal levels of comprehension.

Getting Started

As a rule, the passages in a book designed to improve reading speed should be relatively easy. The student should not have much difficulty with the vocabulary or the subject matter. Don't worry about the passages being too easy; students should see how quickly and efficiently they can read a passage.

Begin by assigning students to a level. A student should start with a book that is one level below his or her current reading level. If a student's reading level is not known, a suitable starting point would be one or two levels below the student's present grade in school.

Introduce students to the contents and format of the book they are using. Examine the book to see how it is organized. Talk about the parts of each lesson. Discuss the purpose of timed reading and the use of the progress graphs at the back of the book.

Timing the Reading

One suggestion for timing the reading is to have all students begin reading the selection at the same time. After one minute, write on the board the time that has elapsed and begin updating it at 10-second intervals (1:00, 1:10, 1:20, etc.). Another option is to have individual students time themselves with a stopwatch.

Teaching a Lesson

Part A

1. Give students the signal to begin previewing the lesson. Allow 20 seconds, then discuss special terms or vocabulary that students found.

2. Use one of the methods described above to time students as they read the passage. (Include the 20-second preview time as part of the first minute.) Tell students to write down the last time shown on the board or the stopwatch when they finish reading. Have them record the time in the designated space after the passage.

3. Next, have students complete the exercises in Part A. Work with them to check their answers, using the Answer Key that begins on page 114. Have them circle incorrect answers, mark the correct answers, and then record the numbers of correct answers for Part A on the appropriate line at the end of the lesson. Correct responses to eight or more questions indicate satisfactory comprehension and recall.

Part B

1. Have students read the Part B passage and complete the exercises that follow it. Directions are provided with each exercise. Correct responses require deliberation and discrimination.

2. Work with students to check their answers. Then discuss the answers with them and have them record the number of correct answers for Part B at the end of the lesson.

Have students study the correct answers to the questions they answered incorrectly. It is important that they understand why a particular answer is correct or incorrect.

Have them reread relevant parts of a passage to clarify an answer. An effective cooperative activity is to have students work in pairs to discuss their answers, explain why they chose the answers they did, and try to resolve differences.

Monitoring Progress

Have students find their total correct answers for the lesson and record their reading time and scores on the graphs on pages 116 and 117. Then have them complete the Comprehension Skills Profile on page 118. For each incorrect response to a question in Part B, students should mark an X in the box above each question type.

The legend on the Reading Rate graph automatically converts reading times to words-per-minute rates. The Comprehension Score graph automatically converts the raw scores to percentages.

These graphs provide a visual record of a student's progress. This record gives the student and you an opportunity to evaluate the student's progress and to determine the types of exercises and skills he or she needs to concentrate on.

Diagnosis and Evaluation

The following are typical reading rates.

Slow Reader—150 Words Per Minute

Average Reader—250 Words Per Minute

Fast Reader—350 Words Per Minute

A student who consistently reads at an average or above-average rate (with satisfactory comprehension) is ready to advance to the next book in the series.

A column of Xs in the Comprehension Skills Profile indicates a specific comprehension weakness. Using the profile, you can assess trends in student performance and suggest remedial work if necessary.

During the 1800s, African Americans worked long days in the fields of the American South. To ease their labor, they sang "field hollers" that they had brought from Africa. One person sang a line. Then a group of workers repeated it. The songs' words told of the hardships that people suffered. This call-and-response singing style was also used in church. African Americans sang "shout spirituals," or joyous religious songs. They clapped their hands and stomped their feet to the music.

After the Civil War, the music changed dramatically. African American music, from ballads to church music, took new forms. It also adapted dance music, called "jump-ups," which had great rhythm. Banjos became popular. A blues singer usually played a call and response with the banjo. He or she sang a line and then played the banjo response. By the early 1900s, the guitar had replaced the banjo as the main blues instrument.

Northern Mississippi—called the Delta—was the center of the blues tradition. By the 1920s, the Delta had many clubs, so-called juke joints. African Americans listened and danced to music in these clubs. Some of the greatest blues men and women performed there.

Blues have a soulful sound that is easy to recognize. The musical notes are often "bent." That is, they are changed slightly to give a song more strength. Whatever their origin, these bent notes most often define the blues.

Lyrics are the words of a song. Blues lyrics describe everyday life. The lyrics, often about relationships between men and women, are often very intense and personal. They tell about sorrow and overwork. They tell about finding or losing love, having money or being broke, being happy or sad and lonely. The lyrics may use humor to describe life's trials and joys. They almost always use the rhythms of everyday speech. A typical blues stanza, or group of lyrics, has three lines. The second line repeats the first line. The third line has different words.

By the 1940s, large numbers of African Americans had left the Delta and moved north to work. Many settled in Chicago. There, a new kind of "electric," or "Chicago," blues began. Many of its themes were the same, but these blues had "wailing" electric guitars and harmonicas. The music had a steady, strong drumbeat. The loud, driving Chicago blues was excellent dance music. Chicago blues led to the birth of a new music style—rock and roll.

Reading Time _____

Recalling Facts

1. The "field holler" is a kind of music that came from
   - ❑ a. the American South.
   - ❑ b. Africa.
   - ❑ c. Chicago.

2. "Shout spirituals" and "field hollers" are similar in that both
   - ❑ a. used banjos.
   - ❑ b. were sung in church.
   - ❑ c. included call-and-response singing.

3. A typical blues stanza is made up of
   - ❑ a. three lines.
   - ❑ b. a harmonica.
   - ❑ c. a driving beat.

4. The Delta, the home of the blues, is located in
   - ❑ a. West Africa.
   - ❑ b. northern Mississippi.
   - ❑ c. Chicago.

5. Chicago blues led to the creation of
   - ❑ a. the harmonica.
   - ❑ b. electric guitars.
   - ❑ c. rock and roll.

Understanding Ideas

6. One can conclude from the passage that the blues
   - ❑ a. would not have flourished without the juke joints of Mississippi.
   - ❑ b. served as a form of communication and self-expression.
   - ❑ c. were successful only in the American South.

7. African Americans probably moved to Chicago because
   - ❑ a. the South was too hot in summer.
   - ❑ b. they liked the Chicago blues.
   - ❑ c. there were more jobs there.

8. Compared with the Delta blues, the Chicago blues
   - ❑ a. were louder and had a more forceful drumbeat.
   - ❑ b. contained lyrics that spoke more often about falling in love.
   - ❑ c. were more heavily influenced by bent notes that came from West African music.

9. Which of the following is an opinion about the blues supported in the passage?
   - ❑ a. Blues focus only on the sadness of everyday life.
   - ❑ b. Blues can communicate a wide range of human emotions.
   - ❑ c. The Delta blues are the only real blues.

10. One can conclude that blues in the United States spread as a result of
    - ❑ a. the work of a single musician.
    - ❑ b. the efforts of many musicians.
    - ❑ c. several well-known musical families from West Africa.

1 B Muddy Waters

McKinley Morganfield was born in 1915 in Mississippi. His mother died when he was three years old. He then went to live with his grandmother in Clarksdale, in the heart of Delta blues country. That was where he got his nickname—Muddy Waters.

Waters loved the blues. At 13 he taught himself how to play the harmonica. By the time he was 17, he had mastered the guitar. Whenever possible, he played music and sang at house parties and with local bands. Waters had a deep, growling voice that expressed intense feeling.

Life for Waters was hard in Mississippi. In 1943 he headed north for Chicago to find work. In Chicago, Waters began playing electric guitar. At first, he played behind other blues musicians. Soon his brilliant guitar playing and powerful voice made him popular. Waters developed his own style—the new electric blues. With his "wailing, shivering" electric guitar and his gritty voice, he became a star. He formed a band, which in 1948 made its first record. The Chicago blues was born.

By 1960 Muddy Waters had made some of the greatest blues recordings ever. The songs he recorded became instant blues classics. His music was peerless; no other musician could match his unique style. Throughout his life, he was truly a king of the blues.

1. **Recognizing Words in Context**

   Find the word *peerless* in the passage. One definition below is closest to the meaning of that word. One definition has the opposite or nearly the opposite meaning. The remaining definition has a completely different meaning. Label the definitions C for *closest*, O for *opposite or nearly opposite*, and D for *different*.

   _____ a. ordinary

   _____ b. without equal

   _____ c. without friends

2. **Distinguishing Fact from Opinion**

   Two of the statements below present *facts*, which can be proved. The other statement is an *opinion*, which expresses someone's thoughts or beliefs. Label the statements F for *fact* and O for *opinion*.

   _____ a. Muddy Waters's real name was McKinley Morganfield.

   _____ b. Muddy Waters's voice expressed the most intense feelings of any blues musician.

   _____ c. Muddy Waters played the electric guitar.

3. Keeping Events in Order

Number the statements below 1, 2, and 3 to show the order in which the events took place.

_____ a. Muddy Waters made his first record.

_____ b. Muddy Waters learned to play the harmonica.

_____ c. Muddy Waters moved to Chicago.

4. Making Correct Inferences

Two of the statements below are correct *inferences,* or reasonable guesses. They are based on information in the passage. The other statement is an incorrect, or faulty, inference. Label the statements C for *correct* inference and F for *faulty* inference.

_____ a. Muddy Waters got his nickname because of his growling voice.

_____ b. Muddy Waters tried out new musical sounds.

_____ c. Muddy Waters believed that Chicago would open up opportunities for him.

5. Understanding Main Ideas

One of the statements below expresses the main idea of the passage. One statement is too general, or too broad. The other explains only part of the passage; it is too narrow. Label the statements M for *main idea,* B for *too broad,* and N for *too narrow.*

_____ a. Muddy Waters played a "wailing" guitar.

_____ b. Muddy Waters created a new blues style.

_____ c. The blues are a popular musical style.

Correct Answers, Part A _____

Correct Answers, Part B _____

Total Correct Answers _____

2 A   The Significance of Harvest: Harvest Festivals

In many parts of the world, harvest festivals are still celebrated. In West Africa, people celebrate the New Yam Festival, called *Iri-ji*. Yams, a kind of sweet potato, are a main food in countries such as Nigeria. There, the Ibo people hold a yam harvest festival each August. The night before the festival, the last year's yams are disposed of. A village elder or chief eats the first new yam and offers the harvest to the gods and the people's ancestors before dividing them among the people. On festival day, the whole village celebrates. Friends and relatives come to share in the feast. The people eat their fill of yams. All day and night, people take part in traditional dances.

The people of South India celebrate a four-day-long festival called Pongal. In this region, the monsoon rains that come in October and November water the crops, which are ready for harvest in January. On the first day of Pongal, the people clean house and give thanks to Indra, ruler of the clouds, for bringing rain. On the second day, they say prayers to Surya, the sun god. They offer him a treat made of rice, herbs, sugarcane, and spices. On the third day, the festival of cattle takes place. Cows receive thanks for pulling plows and giving milk. The people wash the cattle. Then they decorate the horns with colored powder, ribbons, and bells. The cows eat the food prepared for the sun god the day before. The final day is devoted to outdoor activities and excursions. The people also set out rice balls for the birds to eat. This is believed to bring good luck and happiness.

Other places have similarly elaborate harvest rituals. In Brazil, for example, people celebrate Saint John's Day (*São João*). This midwinter festival takes place on June 24–25. (Because Brazil is in the Southern Hemisphere, it is winter there when it is summer in North America.) During *São João,* the people light bonfires to wake up Saint John in heaven to hear the prayers of the people. The festival also involves special foods. People cook desserts made from corn. Among these are *pamonha* (sweet corn mashed and wrapped in cooked husks) and *canjica* (a corn pudding). Young people dress in traditional straw hats and patchwork garments to look like *matutos,* or farm workers.

Where many people are farmers, it is likely that people will continue to celebrate the harvest.

Reading Time _____

Recalling Facts

1. The harvest takes place when
   - ❏ a. crops are planted.
   - ❏ b. crops are gathered.
   - ❏ c. the New Year begins.

2. A yam is a kind of
   - ❏ a. cattle.
   - ❏ b. ceremony.
   - ❏ c. sweet potato.

3. An Ibo chief offers the harvest to the
   - ❏ a. gods and ancestors.
   - ❏ b. elders.
   - ❏ c. guests of the people.

4. During Pongal, cattle are honored because they
   - ❏ a. do farm work to help people.
   - ❏ b. are killed for meat.
   - ❏ c. are sacrificed to the ancestors.

5. The ceremonies of *São João* are held
   - ❏ a. at the end of June.
   - ❏ b. in January, after the monsoons.
   - ❏ c. without ritual foods.

Understanding Ideas

6. Pongal differs from other harvest festivals in that
   - ❏ a. the people do not have a group feast.
   - ❏ b. in it thanks are given to animals.
   - ❏ c. in it thanks are given to gods.

7. From the passage, one can infer that people in South India
   - ❏ a. grow rice.
   - ❏ b. believe in one god.
   - ❏ c. value cows more than people.

8. From the information about the New Yam Festival in the passage, one can assume that the Ibo people
   - ❏ a. do not eat meat.
   - ❏ b. believe that their ancestors help the crops grow.
   - ❏ c. do not share their yams with others.

9. The main idea of this passage is that
   - ❏ a. West Africa, India, and Brazil are the principal areas of the world that celebrate harvest festivals.
   - ❏ b. tradition plays an important role in modern society.
   - ❏ c. people express their thankfulness for a successful harvest in many ways.

10. From the information in the passage, one can conclude that *São João*
    - ❏ a. is a Christian celebration.
    - ❏ b. is performed only if the harvest is abundant.
    - ❏ c. involves purifying oneself by fasting.

2   B   Ch'usok

Ch'usok is the Korean harvest festival. It takes place on the fifteenth day of the eighth lunar month of the year—the time of the harvest moon. The festival takes place about Thanksgiving time in the United States.

On the morning of *Ch'usok*, Koreans worship their ancestors. They visit the graves of loved ones who have died, offering them food from the harvest and asking for their blessings.

Later that day, the whole family makes *songp'yon*, which are scrumptious crescent-shaped rice cakes. The cakes are stuffed with sesame seeds and chestnut paste. Children love *songp'yon*. Often they must wait until evening to eat them. Only after the family has eaten a dinner of rice, fruit, and nuts may the children have *songp'yon*.

Later, people gather for games and dances. Farmers' bands play traditional music. In some parts of Korea, people perform masked and circle dances; in other areas, villages compete in a huge tug-of-war game. The tortoise game is played in other parts of the country. Two men disguise themselves as tortoises and go around the village dancing. The villagers reward them with food and drink.

Whatever form the celebrations take, *Ch'usok* is a time to give thanks for the rice harvest. It is a tradition that binds families, communities, and the Korean nation together.

1. **Recognizing Words in Context**

   Find the word *scrumptious* in the passage. One definition below is closest to the meaning of that word. One definition has the opposite or nearly the opposite meaning. The remaining definition has a completely different meaning. Label the definitions C for *closest*, O for *opposite or nearly opposite*, and D for *different*.

   _____ a. hopeful

   _____ b. delicious

   _____ c. bitter

2. **Distinguishing Fact from Opinion**

   Two of the statements below present *facts*, which can be proved. The other statement is an *opinion*, which expresses someone's thoughts or beliefs. Label the statements F for *fact* and O for *opinion*.

   _____ a. All children enjoy *songp'yon*.

   _____ b. Koreans ask for their ancestors' blessings.

   _____ c. People perform traditional circle dances.

3. Keeping Events in Order

Number the statements below 1, 2, and 3 to show the order in which the events take place.

_____ a. People play a tug-of-war game.

_____ b. People offer food to their ancestors.

_____ c. People make crescent-shaped rice cakes.

4. Making Correct Inferences

Two of the statements below are correct *inferences,* or reasonable guesses. They are based on information in the passage. The other statement is an incorrect, or faulty, inference. Label the statements C for *correct* inference and F for *faulty* inference.

_____ a. *Songp'yon* rice cakes taste sweet.

_____ b. *Ch'usok* is usually celebrated in November.

_____ c. *Ch'usok* is celebrated the same way in all parts of Korea.

5. Understanding Main Ideas

One of the statements below expresses the main idea of the passage. One statement is too general, or too broad. The other explains only part of the passage; it is too narrow. Label the statements M for *main idea,* B for *too broad,* and N for *too narrow.*

_____ a. Harvest festivals are celebrated in many parts of the world.

_____ b. Koreans enjoy doing traditional dances at *Ch'usok.*

_____ c. Koreans celebrate *Ch'usok* with food, games, and dancing.

Correct Answers, Part A _____

Correct Answers, Part B _____

Total Correct Answers _____

The Great Seal of the United States

The Great Seal of the United States is a symbol of the nation's principles. Work on the Great Seal began in 1776. A committee of the Founders of the nation considered several designs before settling on one. The design was changed three times before it was officially declared final in 1782.

The Great Seal has two sides. The main object shown on the front is the bald eagle. This bird is found only in North America. The committee believed that the eagle was a symbol of supreme power and authority and that it signified the Congress. On the seal, the eagle holds two symbols in its talons. In its right talon is an olive branch, a symbol of peace. In its left talon is a bundle of 13 arrows. The arrows symbolize war but also the power of unity. The number 13 represents the 13 colonies. The bundle indicates that united colonies are strong. A shield with 13 red and white stripes covers the eagle's body. The stripes also suggest the 13 colonies. The bald eagle holds a scroll that reads *E pluribus unum*. This is the motto of the United States, meaning "Out of many, one."

On both the front and the back of the seal is an image called "A Glory Breaking Through a Cloud." In this image, glory is shown as rays of light streaming out of a cloud. On the front, the same image is located above the bald eagle's head. On the back, glory is seen streaming outward from a triangle with an eye centered in it.

The back of the seal also includes some mysterious symbols. The main image is of an incomplete pyramid. Its top part is missing. William Barton, who designed this image, said that it signified strength and longevity. No one knows why the pyramid was left unfinished. The great poet Walt Whitman explained its symbolism when he wrote, "The architects of these States laid the foundations. . . . Now are needed other architects. . . . America is not finished, and perhaps never will be."

Above the unfinished pyramid is a triangle. Inside the triangle is the "divine human eye." Its designer explained that this was the eye of Providence in a radiant triangle. Above this image are the Latin words *Annuit Coeptis,* which mean "providence has favored our undertakings." Another Latin phrase, *Novus Ordo Seclorum,* is written below the unfinished pyramid. The English translation of these words is "a new order of the age."

Reading Time _____

Recalling Facts

1. Work on the Great Seal began
   - ❏ a. in 1776.
   - ❏ b. in 1782.
   - ❏ c. after the Revolutionary War.

2. The symbol of the United States is
   - ❏ a. the dollar bill.
   - ❏ b. an eye in a triangle.
   - ❏ c. the bald eagle.

3. The motto of the United States,
   E pluribus unum, means
   - ❏ a. Glory breaks through a cloud.
   - ❏ b. Out of many, one.
   - ❏ c. America is not finished.

4. The main image on the back of the
   seal is
   - ❏ a. the olive branch.
   - ❏ b. a shield having 13 stripes.
   - ❏ c. an unfinished pyramid.

5. The bundle of arrows that the eagle
   holds symbolizes
   - ❏ a. strength in unity.
   - ❏ b. the warlike nature of the nation.
   - ❏ c. a tribute to Native Americans.

Understanding Ideas

6. Both sides of the Great Seal are
   similar in that both show
   - ❏ a. glory breaking through a cloud.
   - ❏ b. the image of a bald eagle.
   - ❏ c. the motto *E pluribus unum.*

7. The bald eagle was chosen for the
   Great Seal and as a symbol of the
   nation because it
   - ❏ a. is a fierce hunter.
   - ❏ b. has authority over other birds.
   - ❏ c. is a powerful bird found only in
     North America.

8. Walt Whitman probably believed that
   the broken pyramid suggested the
   United States as
   - ❏ a. always breaking apart.
   - ❏ b. continually developing.
   - ❏ c. never being a united nation.

9. The reason that the image of a
   pyramid was used to symbolize
   "strength and duration" was
   probably that the pyramids of Egypt
   - ❏ a. have lasted thousands of years.
   - ❏ b. were built by ancient and
     powerful kings.
   - ❏ c. were built by thousands of
     workers.

10. The main idea of this passage is that
    the Great Seal
    - ❏ a. took a long time to design.
    - ❏ b. contains many foreign
      influences.
    - ❏ c. contains symbols of the nation's
      principles.

Opinions differ about how Uncle Sam became a national symbol. He was not created by the government. Uncle Sam is a character that emerged from popular culture.

Some historians believe that he is based on a real person, Samuel Wilson. During the War of 1812, Wilson sold meat to American troops. Wilson labeled the meat barrels *US*. This meant that it was for the army. At that time, *US* was not used to mean "United States." An officer asked what the *US* on the barrels meant. A soldier replied, "Uncle Sam," meaning Samuel Wilson.

The Uncle Sam image today shows a man with a beard, a stars-and-stripes top hat, and a suit. Thomas Nast created this image in about 1838. It represented the government in Nast's political cartoons. Some people believe that Nast based his image on Dan Rice, a popular clown. Rice performed while wearing a star-spangled top hat and suit.

James M. Flagg drew the most famous image of Uncle Sam in 1917, during World War I. It shows a stern man pointing a finger at the viewer. The caption reads "Uncle Sam wants you." Flagg drew this enduring image to encourage Americans to join the U.S. Army. It has been used for this purpose ever since.

Today, Uncle Sam is a symbol of the United States that is recognized around the world.

1. **Recognizing Words in Context**

   Find the word *enduring* in the passage. One definition below is closest to the meaning of that word. One definition has the opposite or nearly the opposite meaning. The remaining definition has a completely different meaning. Label the definitions C for *closest*, O for *opposite or nearly opposite*, and D for *different*.

   _____ a. fleeting

   _____ b. long-lasting

   _____ c. painful

2. **Distinguishing Fact from Opinion**

   Two of the statements below present *facts*, which can be proved. The other statement is an *opinion*, which expresses someone's thoughts or beliefs. Label the statements F for *fact* and O for *opinion*.

   _____ a. Samuel Wilson sold meat to the army.

   _____ b. The Uncle Sam symbol is the best of all American symbols.

   _____ c. Uncle Sam is a symbol of the United States that is recognized around the world.

3. **Keeping Events in Order**

Number the statements below 1, 2, and 3 to show the order in which the events took place.

_____ a. Thomas Nast drew the first picture of Uncle Sam.

_____ b. Soldiers said that the label *US* meant "Uncle Sam."

_____ c. James Flagg drew a picture of Uncle Sam to urge people to join the Army.

4. **Making Correct Inferences**

Two of the statements below are correct *inferences,* or reasonable guesses. They are based on information in the passage. The other statement is an incorrect, or faulty, inference. Label the statements C for *correct* inference and F for *faulty* inference.

_____ a. Uncle Sam's star-spangled hat and suit reflect the American flag.

_____ b. Samuel Wilson was a businessman during the War of 1812.

_____ c. Uncle Sam was based on a clown to show that Americans were humorous people.

5. **Understanding Main Ideas**

One of the statements below expresses the main idea of the passage. One statement is too general, or too broad. The other explains only part of the passage; it is too narrow. Label the statements M for *main idea,* B for *too broad,* and N for *too narrow.*

_____ a. The name Uncle Sam was invented during the War of 1812.

_____ b. There are many symbols of the United States, including Uncle Sam.

_____ c. Over time, the image of Uncle Sam came to represent the United States.

Correct Answers, Part A _____

Correct Answers, Part B _____

Total Correct Answers _____

The Ice Age in North America

A long period of time in which sheets of ice cover much of Earth's surface is called an ice age. There have been several ice ages. The first began more than 500 million years ago. The last one ended about 10,000 years ago. It covered North America with a layer of ice 1.2 to 2 miles thick.

The sheets of ice are known as glaciers. Glaciers form when winter snow does not melt completely in the summer. As more snow falls, it turns the old snow underneath into ice. People might think it is always cold during an ice age. In fact, the climate can be both warm and cold. As climate changes, the huge sheets of ice begin to melt and then freeze again. This causes them to move back and forth.

The moving glaciers pick up sand and other debris. They carry those with them until they melt in a warmer climate. The debris they leave behind forms large hills of clay, stones, or sand. As they move, the heavy glaciers also scrape the ground below them. Melting water fills the gouges that the traveling glaciers make. These gouges form lakes, bays, and other bodies of water.

The impact of this glacial movement is easy to see in North America. When glaciers scraped away tons of soil in what is now Michigan, they formed the gaps that made the Great Lakes. Niagara Falls is just one of the amazing landmarks that glaciers made. Glaciers even had an impact in regions that were not actually covered in ice. For example, glacial ice never reached the Delaware Peninsula, but melting ice from other places flooded a valley that became Delaware Bay.

Ice age glaciers influenced living things too. In the extreme cold, large furry creatures, such as the woolly mammoth, developed. The largest animals survived longest. Most died out. Changes in the animal kingdom continued when the climate warmed and the glaciers retreated. Some animals that had thrived in the cold became extinct.

At some time during this period, our human ancestors appeared. The discovery of early tools from the Ice Age leads to this conclusion. As the glacial waters left, the first true civilizations began.

Scientists think that Earth is now in a warm period between ice ages. Some believe that the next one will come in about 23,000 years. Others say it might begin just 1,000 years from now.

Reading Time _____

Recalling Facts

1. The last ice age ended about
   - ❏ a. 500 million years ago.
   - ❏ b. 10,000 years ago.
   - ❏ c. 10 million years ago.

2. Glaciers form because
   - ❏ a. sheets of water cover the earth and then freeze.
   - ❏ b. the land is at low altitude.
   - ❏ c. winter snow does not melt completely and builds up.

3. Melting water from glaciers creates _____ in gouges.
   - ❏ a. new oceans
   - ❏ b. lakes and bays
   - ❏ c. streams

4. The cold climate provided a good environment for
   - ❏ a. small amphibians.
   - ❏ b. all mammals.
   - ❏ c. woolly mammoths.

5. The Ice Age affected animals and human beings differently in that
   - ❏ a. furry animals grew smaller while human beings grew larger.
   - ❏ b. large, woolly animals developed while other animals died out.
   - ❏ c. animals thrived in the cold, while human beings did not.

Understanding Ideas

6. From the passage, one can infer that our human ancestors
   - ❏ a. did not know how to use tools.
   - ❏ b. had sophisticated civilizations.
   - ❏ c. were able to survive in a cold climate.

7. One can conclude from the passage that
   - ❏ a. glaciers affected every area on Earth.
   - ❏ b. glaciers affected vast areas of North America.
   - ❏ c. glaciers affected only the midwestern United States.

8. One can conclude that
   - ❏ a. Earth is not likely to have another ice age.
   - ❏ b. civilization will not survive a new ice age.
   - ❏ c. animals must adapt to changes in climate or become extinct.

9. From the passage, one can infer that ice age climates
   - ❏ a. are frigid.
   - ❏ b. are windy.
   - ❏ c. vary.

10. Which of the following statements best summarizes the main idea of the passage?
    - ❏ a. Ice age glaciers had a widespread impact on North American geography and life-forms.
    - ❏ b. Long periods known as ice ages are part of Earth's climate history.
    - ❏ c. The most recent ice age covered North America with a layer of ice about two miles thick.

The Finger Lakes of New York State

The Finger Lakes of upstate New York are a group of 11 lakes. They run from north to south and look like outstretched human fingers. Scientists say that ice age glaciers formed them over the last 2 million years.

The Finger Lakes were once rivers. During the Pleistocene era, a huge ice cap formed. This took place sometime between 1.8 million and 11,000 years ago. As glaciers moved across the rivers, they carved deep trenches. When the ice cap melted, water filled those holes to form the Finger Lakes.

The longest of the lakes is Lake Cayuga. It stretches more than 38 miles. It is one of the deepest lakes in North America. The hole that the glaciers first carved was probably even deeper. Over time, some of the lake filled with silt that the glaciers carried with them.

There are other signs that glaciers were in the area. At the southern ends of the Finger Lakes are deposits of gravel called moraines. There are also long hills, called drumlins, made of debris that moving glaciers left behind. Throughout the Finger Lakes region, the ice age left many traces, from a section of prehistoric sea floor at Watkins Glen State Park to the small waterfalls made as glacial water ran down walls of rock into the lakes.

1. **Recognizing Words in Context**

   Find the word *trenches* in the passage. One definition below is closest to the meaning of that word. One definition has the opposite or nearly the opposite meaning. The remaining definition has a completely different meaning. Label the definitions C for *closest,* O for *opposite or nearly opposite,* and D for *different.*

   _____ a. hills

   _____ b. plains

   _____ c. holes

2. **Distinguishing Fact from Opinion**

   Two of the statements below present *facts,* which can be proved. The other statement is an *opinion,* which expresses someone's thoughts or beliefs. Label the statements F for *fact* and O for *opinion.*

   _____ a. The Finger Lakes were once rivers.

   _____ b. Lake Cayuga is the most beautiful of the Finger Lakes.

   _____ c. The Finger Lakes region shows evidence of ice age glacial movement.

3. Keeping Events in Order

Number the statements below 1, 2, and 3 to show the order in which the events took place.

_____ a. Rivers formed in the Finger Lakes region.

_____ b. Sediment collected at the bottom of Lake Cayuga.

_____ c. Glaciers carved holes in the earth.

4. Making Correct Inferences

Two of the statements below are correct *inferences,* or reasonable guesses. They are based on information in the passage. The other statement is an incorrect, or faulty, inference. Label the statements C for *correct* inference and F for *faulty* inference.

_____ a. Glaciers can create both holes and hills.

_____ b. All of the lakes in North America were made by glaciers.

_____ c. Climate changes can cause changes in Earth's surface.

5. Understanding Main Ideas

One of the statements below expresses the main idea of the passage. One statement is too general, or too broad. The other explains only part of the passage; it is too narrow. Label the statements M for *main idea,* B for *too broad,* and N for *too narrow.*

_____ a. The Finger Lakes and other nearby geological features are the result of glacial events.

_____ b. During the Ice Age, glaciers formed lakes and hills in North America.

_____ c. The longest of the Finger Lakes is Lake Cayuga.

Correct Answers, Part A _____

Correct Answers, Part B _____

Total Correct Answers _____

Lewis and Clark and Their Relations with Native Americans

In May 1804, President Thomas Jefferson asked Meriwether Lewis and William Clark to lead an expedition west of the Mississippi River. They were to find a route to the Pacific Coast. On the way, they met many Native American peoples. Lewis and Clark explained that the Native people's land was now part of the United States.

The encounters began in July 1804, when the expedition first came upon the buffalo-hunting Missouri Nation. Lewis and Clark gave the Missouri gifts.

Later that summer, the explorers encountered Mandan villages on the Upper Missouri River. The Mandan were friendly. They gave the explorers food and shelter for the winter.

In October the explorers met the Arikaras. The Arikaras hunted buffalo, but they were mainly farmers. They made trade pacts with the explorers. Soon after, the party arrived at a Hidatsa village, where the group met Sacagawea. She traveled with the party as a translator.

The explorers next met the Teton Sioux. The Sioux were not moved by Lewis and Clark's promise of peace. Rather, they believed that the group wanted to control trade. Growing tensions nearly ended in violence. The Teton chief stepped in to prevent fighting. After three days, repeated conflicts forced Lewis and Clark to leave.

In August 1805, the party encountered the Shoshone, who gathered food and hunted small game. They were fearful at first, but Lewis's gestures of peace and the gifts he brought put them at ease. The explorers bought horses from the Shoshone for the trip across the mountains. In exchange Lewis promised to bring guns to help the Shoshone hunt.

In the fall of 1805, the expedition met the Walla Walla people. The chief welcomed the party. He gave Clark a gift of a white horse. At a tribal feast, the chief told the explorers how to reach the Nez Perce.

The Nez Perce lived west of the Rocky Mountains. They welcomed the expedition and sought to trade with members for hunting guns and ammunition. The explorers interacted well with the Nez Perce.

Next, the explorers met the Blackfoot. Lewis told them that nearby Native nations had accepted peace and were given guns. The Blackfoot were angry that their enemies had weapons. A few tried to steal guns from the expedition. This incident led to a fight. One Blackfoot warrior was killed. This was the first blood shed during the expedition. From that time, the Blackfoot were hostile toward whites.

Reading Time _____

Recalling Facts

1. The purpose of Lewis and Clark's expedition was to
   - ❏ a. trade with Native Americans.
   - ❏ b. find a route to the Pacific.
   - ❏ c. cure Native Americans of smallpox.

2. The president who sent Lewis and Clark on their expedition was
   - ❏ a. George Washington.
   - ❏ b. Benjamin Franklin.
   - ❏ c. Thomas Jefferson.

3. The Mandan showed friendliness to the explorers by
   - ❏ a. sheltering them for the winter.
   - ❏ b. giving them horses as gifts.
   - ❏ c. trading their corn with them.

4. The expedition's relationship with the Blackfoot was harmed when
   - ❏ a. the explorers stole horses from them.
   - ❏ b. a Blackfoot warrior was killed in a fight.
   - ❏ c. the Blackfoot were given guns.

5. The Teton Sioux were
   - ❏ a. suspicious of Lewis and Clark.
   - ❏ b. suffering from smallpox.
   - ❏ c. longtime traders with whites.

Understanding Ideas

6. From the information in the passage, one can conclude that the Shoshone
   - ❏ a. were angry with the explorers.
   - ❏ b. had conquered their neighbors.
   - ❏ c. wanted a peaceful relationship with the Lewis and Clark expedition.

7. From the passage, one can conclude that the relationships between the Lewis and Clark expedition and Native nations
   - ❏ a. were always hostile.
   - ❏ b. were always peaceful.
   - ❏ c varied according to the groups and circumstances.

8. The Missouri and the Arikara peoples were similar in that both
   - ❏ a. lived near large rivers.
   - ❏ b. had fought against the Shoshone.
   - ❏ c. hunted buffalo.

9. From the information in the passage, one can infer that the Blackfoot
   - ❏ a. did not accept white settlement peacefully.
   - ❏ b. were driven from their home in Montana.
   - ❏ c. stole guns from the Nez Perce people.

10. One can infer from the information in the passage that the Arikara people
    - ❏ a. gave the explorers buffalo hides.
    - ❏ b. lived in farming villages.
    - ❏ c. died from lack of buffalo on the plains.

Sacagawea was a Shoshone. When she was 12 years old, the Hidatsa people kidnapped her. They took her away from her home in what today is Idaho. They brought her East. There they sold her to a French-Canadian fur trader, Toussaint Charbonneau. She became his wife.

In November 1804, the Lewis-and-Clark party arrived at the Hidatsa village, where they built a fort. In 1805 Sacagawea gave birth to a son. She spoke the languages of the Hidatsa and the Shoshone, and Charbonneau spoke Hidatsa and French. Together, Clark thought, they would be valuable as translators as the party moved west.

Sacagawea was the only woman in the party. She was a good translator and was skilled at finding edible plants and roots to eat when meat was scarce. She carried her son on her back. The boy pleased the explorers. They called him "Pompy," which means "little dancing boy."

In 1805 the party met Sacagawea's Shoshone band. Her brother had become their chief. The reunion was a happy one, and the party stayed for several days. Then Sacagawea left the expedition.

Sacagawea helped the explorers in many ways. She was an excellent guide. She helped lead the party through the wild country and kept them safe. Many Native people had never seen whites before. Sacagawea was able to assure them that the whites were friendly.

1. **Recognizing Words in Context**

   Find the word *edible* in the passage. One definition below is closest to the meaning of that word. One definition has the opposite or nearly the opposite meaning. The remaining definition has a completely different meaning. Label the definitions C for *closest,* O for *opposite or nearly opposite,* and D for *different.*

   _____ a. poisonous

   _____ b. safe to eat

   _____ c. cooked well

2. **Distinguishing Fact from Opinion**

   Two of the statements below present *facts,* which can be proved. The other statement is an *opinion,* which expresses someone's thoughts or beliefs. Label the statements F for *fact* and O for *opinion.*

   _____ a. The explorers called the boy Pompy.

   _____ b. Sacagawea could speak Hidatsa.

   _____ c. Sacagawea had the most useful skills of anyone on the expedition.

3. Keeping Events in Order

Number the statements below 1, 2, and 3 to show the order in which the events took place.

_____ a. Sacagawea went west with the expedition.

_____ b. Sacagawea was kidnapped by the Hidatsa.

_____ c. Sacagawea gave birth to a son.

4. Making Correct Inferences

Two of the statements below are correct *inferences,* or reasonable guesses. They are based on information in the passage. The other statement is an incorrect, or faulty, inference. Label the statements C for *correct* inference and F for *faulty* inference.

_____ a. As an adult, Sacagawea stopped missing her family and people.

_____ b. Sacagawea spoke to her husband in the Hidatsa language.

_____ c. Having a child on the expedition was no great hardship for the explorers.

5. Understanding Main Ideas

One of the statements below expresses the main idea of the passage. One statement is too general, or too broad. The other explains only part of the passage; it is too narrow. Label the statements M for *main idea,* B for *too broad,* and N for *too narrow.*

_____ a. Sacagawea was a valuable translator and helper for the explorers.

_____ b. Sacagawea spoke Hidatsa and Shoshone.

_____ c. Native American women such as Sacagawea and Pocahontas have an important place in history.

Correct Answers, Part A _____

Correct Answers, Part B _____

Total Correct Answers _____

6   A   The Social Impact of Television

Television first became popular in the 1940s. Then TV brought people together. They gathered in the home of the lucky neighbor who owned a set. TV still has social impacts. Some of them are positive, but some are negative.

Today TV often isolates people. In many American homes, every family member has a TV set in the bedroom. Each watches his or her own programs. There is less interaction with family and friends. Some medical experts believe that TV is bad for a person's health. Many Americans are "couch potatoes." They do little more than sit around watching TV.

On the positive side, people can get breaking news on TV around the clock. When they learn how people live in other parts of the world, they can better understand global problems. Some channels bring excellent music, dance, and drama into the home. The benefits of TV are not all highbrow, though. TV also provides entertainment and escape, things that everyone needs and enjoys.

However, some critics claim that too much escape is harmful. It numbs the mind. Obsessive viewers lose interest in the "real world." The world shown on TV is often not the one real people live in. Often, the TV world is idealized. Ads strive to sell products that appear in this make-believe TV world to people who cannot afford them. Too often, the views of a show's sponsor dictate the content. Sponsors want to appeal to a broad audience. This tends to make the programs bland. Few sponsors are willing to take a chance on new, groundbreaking programs.

On the plus side, television is good for democracy. Candidate debates are shown before most elections. Election results are broadcast as soon as they are available. However, political ads are not free. TV channels sell time to candidates, so the candidate with the most money may have an unfair advantage.

The content of TV programs often generates controversy. For example, programs sometimes stereotype people, especially minority groups. Such generalizing may affect the way viewers see minorities. TV violence, however, is open to the most content criticism. Programmers insist that "violence sells." The more violence a show has, the more people watch it. Opponents counter that TV violence is not like real-world violence. Violence on TV rarely has consequences. Some experts fear that it may arouse people, especially children, into committing violent acts.

Reading Time _____

Recalling Facts

1. Television first became popular in the
   - ❑ a. 1940s.
   - ❑ b. 1950s.
   - ❑ c. 1970s.

2. One benefit of today's TV news is that it
   - ❑ a. has no commercials.
   - ❑ b. may be reported as it happens.
   - ❑ c. is available only on cable TV.

3. TV violence is not like real-world violence, because
   - ❑ a. more people are killed on TV.
   - ❑ b. TV violence rarely has consequences.
   - ❑ c. nobody gets hurt on TV.

4. TV benefits a democracy, because candidates
   - ❑ a. show their ads free of charge.
   - ❑ b. are not stereotyped.
   - ❑ c. debate publicly for voters to see.

5. The content of a TV program is often determined by
   - ❑ a. the show's sponsor.
   - ❑ b. a vote by viewers.
   - ❑ c. how much the content resembles the real world.

Understanding Ideas

6. Compared with the 1940s, watching TV today is probably
   - ❑ a. less frequent.
   - ❑ b. more isolating.
   - ❑ c. more social.

7. From the information in the passage, one can infer that most Americans
   - ❑ a. watch TV for entertainment and information.
   - ❑ b. get information about political candidates only through TV.
   - ❑ c. do not enjoy watching TV.

8. The author of this passage would probably agree that TV is
   - ❑ a. mostly a good influence on society.
   - ❑ b. mostly a bad influence on society.
   - ❑ c. both a good and a bad influence on society.

9. From the information in the passage, it is possible to infer that
   - ❑ a. political candidates with the most TV ads always win elections.
   - ❑ b. the government should regulate television programming more strictly.
   - ❑ c. watching too much TV may be harmful.

10. The information in the passage suggests that TV ads
    - ❑ a. fail to sell products.
    - ❑ b. try to influence the way people spend money, sometimes in unfair ways.
    - ❑ c. are clever and often better than the TV show itself.

Television can have both positive and negative effects on children. This conclusion is based on years of research. Children do not just enjoy watching TV. They also learn from it. Some programs can have a positive impact. On the other hand, too much TV and certain types of programs may cause harm.

Educational programs for preschool children can have a very positive influence. Studies show that children who watch them have a head start in school. Many enter already knowing letters and numbers. Some know whole words. Children learn them from TV shows. These children often read early and well. They frequently do better in school than children who do not watch educational TV. Studies also show that children who watch such programs tend to get along better with other children than those who do not.

However, children also watch shows that contain violence. Such shows may harm them. By age 18, most children will have seen 200,000 violent acts on TV. Research shows that children who spend large amounts of time watching violent TV do not interact as well with other children as those who do not watch so much. Experts state that violent programs may make children more aggressive. Also, watching TV can take children's time away from homework. Children who watch too much TV are likely to get lower grades in school.

1. **Recognizing Words in Context**

   Find the word *aggressive* in the passage. One definition below is closest to the meaning of that word. One definition has the opposite or nearly the opposite meaning. The remaining definition has a completely different meaning. Label the definitions C for *closest*, O for *opposite or nearly opposite*, and D for *different*.

   _____ a. hostile

   _____ b. gentle

   _____ c. masculine

2. **Distinguishing Fact from Opinion**

   Two of the statements below present *facts*, which can be proved. The other statement is an *opinion*, which expresses someone's thoughts or beliefs. Label the statements F for *fact* and O for *opinion*.

   _____ a. Children should not be allowed to watch TV.

   _____ b. There are many educational shows on TV.

   _____ c. Some educational programs help children to learn about letters and numbers.

3. Keeping Events in Order

Two of the statements below describe events that happened at the same time. The other statement describes an event that happened before or after those events. Label them S for *same time*, B for *before*, and A for *after*.

_____ a. Children watch educational programs.

_____ b. Children enter school and learn to read.

_____ c. Children learn the letters of the alphabet.

4. Making Correct Inferences

Two of the statements below are correct *inferences*, or reasonable guesses. They are based on information in the passage. The other statement is an incorrect, or faulty, inference. Label the statements C for *correct* inference and F for *faulty* inference.

_____ a. Children learn many things from TV.

_____ b. Most researchers believe that children should not watch TV.

_____ c. Children who watch large amounts of violent TV may become aggressive.

5. Understanding Main Ideas

One of the statements below expresses the main idea of the passage. One statement is too general, or too broad. The other explains only part of the passage; it is too narrow. Label the statements M for *main idea*, B for *too broad*, and N for *too narrow*.

_____ a. Some children watch an excessive amount of TV.

_____ b. Children can benefit from TV, but TV can also have negative effects.

_____ c. Researchers study children and their interests in TV programs.

Correct Answers, Part A _____

Correct Answers, Part B _____

Total Correct Answers _____

From a Bill to a Law

The draft version of a proposed law is called a bill. Only the United States Congress can introduce bills and pass laws. There are two houses of Congress, the House of Representatives and the Senate. A bill must get a majority vote in both to become law. Passing a bill is not easy. Read this example of how an education bill is managed.

First, a member of Congress introduces the bill. Then it is sent to a committee in the House and another in the Senate. Both committees specialize in education issues and laws. These committees may or may not consider the bill. Committee members decide which bills to consider.

If members decide to consider the bill, a committee may hold public hearings. Education experts and concerned citizens will share their expertise, offer advice, and answer questions. After the hearings, committee members hold a "mark-up" session. There, committee members make changes in the bill. Then they vote on whether to send the bill to the full Congress.

If they do send the bill to Congress, there is no rule that forces Congress to consider it. That is up to the leaders of the majority political party—the Speaker of the House and the Senate Majority Leader. If party leaders decide to consider the education bill, it is debated separately in each house of Congress. Members of each house may make changes. In time, all of the changes are made. The members of each house vote on the revised version of the bill. If it gets a majority vote in both houses, it passes.

The bill passed by the House is likely to be somewhat different from the bill passed by the Senate. The two bills must be reconciled. That is, their differences must be resolved. So the two versions are sent to a conference committee. This committee has members from both houses of Congress. The members decide on a final acceptable version of the bill. The compromise bill is voted on again by all members of each house. If it gets a majority vote in both houses of Congress, the bill passes.

Finally the bill is sent to the president to sign. If the president signs it, the bill becomes law. However, the president may veto, or refuse to sign, the bill. Then the bill can become law only if two-thirds of the members of both houses of Congress vote to override the president's veto.

Reading Time _____

Recalling Facts

1. A bill is
   - ❏ a. a house of Congress.
   - ❏ b. the law of the land.
   - ❏ c. a draft of a law.

2. An introduced bill is first considered
   - ❏ a. in an election.
   - ❏ b. by a committee.
   - ❏ c. by a political party.

3. In the lawmaking process, public hearings allow the committee to
   - ❏ a. receive advice.
   - ❏ b. debate the bill.
   - ❏ c. stop the bill.

4. After a bill has been passed by both houses of Congress, it
   - ❏ a. is scheduled for hearings.
   - ❏ b. is presented to the president for a signature.
   - ❏ c. becomes law.

5. A president's veto of a bill means that
   - ❏ a. the bill must go back to a committee.
   - ❏ b. the bill will never become law.
   - ❏ c. the president has refused to sign it.

Understanding Ideas

6. If a bill is never debated on the floor of either house of Congress, one can conclude that it
   - ❏ a. was never introduced.
   - ❏ b. was not brought to either floor of Congress.
   - ❏ c. did not get a two-thirds majority vote in Congress.

7. From the passage, one can infer that passing a bill
   - ❏ a. is usually time consuming but easy.
   - ❏ b. rarely happens because of the complex process involved.
   - ❏ c. requires negotiation and compromise.

8. One can assume that seats on a conference committee are fiercely fought over because the members
   - ❏ a. determine the final version of the bill.
   - ❏ b. have no limits to debate.
   - ❏ c. have the power to veto the bill.

9. Which of the following words best sums up the process of turning a bill into a law?
   - ❏ a. efficient
   - ❏ b. time consuming
   - ❏ c. impossible

10. The process by which a bill becomes a law is a good example of democracy at work in that
    - ❏ a. citizens are able to vote on the bill before it becomes law.
    - ❏ b. very few laws are passed to hinder citizens' rights.
    - ❏ c. bills are considered and debated by all elected representatives in the Congress.

What Is THOMAS?

Citizens in a democracy should know what their government is doing. That is why, in 1995, Congress started THOMAS. Named after President Thomas Jefferson, THOMAS is an Internet data source. It is a Web site about bills, laws, and Congress.

THOMAS is probably the best place on the Web to find information about the lawmaking process. It has data about recently introduced bills and where in the lawmaking process a bill is. For instance, a searcher can use THOMAS to find out whether a bill is in committee. THOMAS can tell users whether a bill has moved to the floor of the House or the Senate. It can tell them whether a bill has moved on to a conference committee. By using THOMAS, a searcher can find out whether a bill has become law. People can also find out whether the person they elected to Congress voted for, voted against, or sponsored a bill. If the representative sponsored it, the person favors it.

THOMAS makes it easy to find a bill. Users can search by name, number, subject, or date on which the bill was introduced.

THOMAS is not just a source of current facts. It is also a good history source. It has facts about laws passed in prior years. In fact, THOMAS contains data about laws passed as long ago as 1774.

1. **Recognizing Words in Context**

   Find the word *sponsored* in the passage. One definition below is closest to the meaning of that word. One definition has the opposite or nearly the opposite meaning. The remaining definition has a completely different meaning. Label the definitions C for *closest,* O for *opposite or nearly opposite,* and D for *different.*

   _____ a. opposed

   _____ b. supported

   _____ c. debated

2. **Distinguishing Fact from Opinion**

   Two of the statements below present *facts,* which can be proved. The other statement is an *opinion,* which expresses someone's thoughts or beliefs. Label the statements F for *fact* and O for *opinion.*

   _____ a. There are a variety of ways to locate a bill on THOMAS.

   _____ b. THOMAS is the best place on the Web to find information about current bills.

   _____ c. THOMAS allows users to search for a bill by subject.

3. Keeping Events in Order

Number the statements below 1, 2, and 3 to show the order in which the events take place.

_____ a. A bill is introduced.

_____ b. A bill is passed into law.

_____ c. A bill is in committee.

4. Making Correct Inferences

Two of the statements below are correct *inferences,* or reasonable guesses. They are based on information in the passage. The other statement is an incorrect, or faulty, inference. Label the statements C for *correct* inference and F for *faulty* inference.

_____ a. Users can find information about state laws on THOMAS.

_____ b. If users know what a bill is about, they can search for it on THOMAS.

_____ c. THOMAS can tell users about laws passed in 1920.

5. Understanding Main Ideas

One of the statements below expresses the main idea of the passage. One statement is too general, or too broad. The other explains only part of the passage; it is too narrow. Label the statements M for *main idea,* B for *too broad,* and N for *too narrow.*

_____ a. Internet Web sites make much information about government policies available to citizens.

_____ b. THOMAS is an Internet data source that offers up-to-date information about bills in Congress.

_____ c. THOMAS lets users search for bills by number.

Correct Answers, Part A _____

Correct Answers, Part B _____

Total Correct Answers _____

King Tutankhamun

More than 3,300 years ago, Tutankhamun became king, or pharaoh, of Egypt. Before Tutankhamun became king, two of his relatives ruled. Their reigns were noted for religious conflict. One of them made a terrible mistake. He banned the worship of all gods except Aten, the sun god. The Egyptians were furious. Egypt's priests fiercely opposed the king's one-god religion. They encouraged people to rise up against him.

When the ruling king died, nine-year-old Tutankhamun became pharaoh. As king he had little power. In fact, he was in grave danger. Nearly all of his relatives were dead. He was under the care of high-level "advisors," who controlled him like a puppet. The land was in turmoil. After Tutankhamun was crowned, the traditional religion was restored. Egyptians again worshiped many gods. Most experts think that the boy king had little to do with this revival. He may even have retained his belief in Aten alone. This may have led to his downfall.

Little is known about "King Tut's" reign other than that it was short. He died when he was 17 or 18 years old. He had an elaborate burial in the Valley of the Kings.

For years rumors circulated about the existence of King Tut's tomb. In 1925 archaeologist Howard Carter located it in the valley. Carefully digging into the ground, Carter unearthed one of the richest tombs ever found. A nest of three coffins surrounded the mummified king. The outer coffin was made of red quartzite stone. The inner coffin was wood covered with gold. The most inner coffin, which held the mummy, was of solid gold. The mummy itself was in poor condition. However, its head was covered by a magnificent gold mask.

Today, the phrase *King Tut* is used to refer to a person of great wealth. Indeed, the pharaoh's tomb held priceless objects of sublime beauty. These included gold bracelets, anklets, collars, and pendants. Chairs, boxes, and chests were of gilded carved wood. These riches are among the most famous artifacts in the world.

Ever since the tomb was opened, people have wondered how the king died. For decades experts believed that he had died of tuberculosis. In 1968 X-rays of the mummy showed that the skull was broken. The pharaoh had been killed by a severe blow to the head. Most historians now believe that King Tut was murdered by one of his advisors: the next in line for the throne.

Reading Time _____

Recalling Facts

1. King Tutankhamun ruled in Egypt about _____ years ago.
   - ❏ a. 1,000
   - ❏ b. 2,500
   - ❏ c. 3,300

2. One of the kings who ruled Egypt before Tutankhamun angered the citizens when he
   - ❏ a. forbade the worship of any god but Aten, the sun god.
   - ❏ b. encouraged people to rise up against the priests.
   - ❏ c. became too rich and powerful.

3. Tutankhamun became pharaoh when he was _____ years old.
   - ❏ a. 33
   - ❏ b. 18
   - ❏ c. 9

4. As king, Tutankhamun was controlled by
   - ❏ a. the priests.
   - ❏ b. his advisors.
   - ❏ c. his closest friends.

5. X-rays in 1968 showed that King Tutankhamun had
   - ❏ a. been killed by a severe blow to the head.
   - ❏ b. died of tuberculosis.
   - ❏ c. broken his arm as a child.

Understanding Ideas

6. From the information in the passage, one can assume that the two kings who ruled before Tutankhamun were similar in that they both
   - ❏ a. had many advisors.
   - ❏ b. had conflicts with the priests.
   - ❏ c. believed in one god.

7. One can infer that Tutankhamun's life was in danger because
   - ❏ a. the kingdom was unstable after many years of conflict.
   - ❏ b. the kingdom was in trouble economically.
   - ❏ c. Tutankhamun was very sickly and weak.

8. An indication that Tutankhamun was respected as Egypt's king is
   - ❏ a. his restoration of traditional religion.
   - ❏ b. his elaborate royal burial.
   - ❏ c. the counsel he received from many advisors.

9. From the description of King Tutankhamun's tomb in the passage, one can infer that
   - ❏ a. tuberculosis was common in ancient Egypt.
   - ❏ b. Egyptian artisans had only a few materials to work with.
   - ❏ c. ancient Egyptians greatly valued gold.

10. The information in the passage suggests that the objects in King Tutankhamun's tomb
    - ❏ a. deserve the high esteem given them.
    - ❏ b. are beautiful but overvalued.
    - ❏ c. are not well preserved.

Imhotep and the Step Pyramid of Djoser

One of the earliest major stone works of ancient Egypt is the complex that includes the Step Pyramid of Djoser. Djoser (or Zoser) was the second king of the third Egyptian dynasty. He was the pharaoh about 4,500 years ago.

The Step Pyramid was to be Djoser's tomb. It was created by a brilliant and powerful man named Imhotep. He was called sage, doctor, and high priest. Imhotep designed and oversaw the building of the tomb. It was the first of its kind to be built out of stone. The tombs of earlier pharaohs had been built of mud brick or wood.

When first begun, Djoser's tomb was a small chamber 92 feet underground. The burial chamber had beautiful blue tiles. It also contained a statue of the pharaoh. A three-ton boulder covered the tomb's entrance. After building the king's tomb, Imhotep extended the underground complex. He added rooms, corridors, and galleries. Then Imhotep built the pyramid above the tomb.

The pyramid was built in several stages. First, two stories were built to contain the tombs of Djoser's family. After that, the *tiers*, or stories, were constructed. Each story is one step. The six enormous stone steps lead to the top of the pyramid. The tomb is 197 feet high. More than 200,000 tons of stone were used to build it.

1. **Recognizing Words in Context**

   Find the word *brilliant* in the passage. One definition below is closest to the meaning of that word. One definition has the opposite or nearly the opposite meaning. The remaining definition has a completely different meaning. Label the definitions C for *closest*, O for *opposite or nearly opposite*, and D for *different*.

   _____ a. intelligent

   _____ b. stupid

   _____ c. ugly

2. **Distinguishing Fact from Opinion**

   Two of the statements below present *facts*, which can be proved. The other statement is an *opinion*, which expresses someone's thoughts or beliefs. Label the statements F for *fact* and O for *opinion*.

   _____ a. Imhotep was the most important leader of ancient Egypt.

   _____ b. The tomb held a statue of the king.

   _____ c. The pyramid has six steps.

3. Keeping Events in Order

Number the sentences below 1, 2, and 3 to show the order in which the events took place.

_____ a. The underground complex was extended.

_____ b. The pharaoh's tomb was built.

_____ c. The pyramid's steps were constructed.

4. Making Correct Inferences

Two of the statements below are correct *inferences,* or reasonable guesses. They are based on information in the passage. The other statement is an incorrect, or faulty, inference. Label the statements C for *correct* inference and F for *faulty* inference.

_____ a. Imhotep was a fine architect.

_____ b. It took many years to build the Step Pyramid.

_____ c. The Step Pyramid is the largest of the Egyptian pyramids.

5. Understanding Main Ideas

One of the statements below expresses the main idea of the passage. One statement is too general, or too broad. The other explains only part of the passage; it is too narrow. Label the statements M for *main idea,* B for *too broad,* and N for *too narrow.*

_____ a. The Step Pyramid has six huge steps.

_____ b. Pyramids were constructed in Egypt.

_____ c. Imhotep built the first stone pyramid, the Step Pyramid, in several stages.

Correct Answers, Part A _____

Correct Answers, Part B _____

Total Correct Answers _____

The History of Soccer

An early form of a game in which a ball was kicked around a field is recorded in 1004 B.C. Japan. Some sports historians believe that the game of soccer began in England in the third century, however. They claim that early English warriors kicked around the head of a defeated enemy. This may or may not be true, but it is certain that soccer is an ancient sport.

Without doubt, the English played soccer during the reign of King Edward I in the 1300s. In fact, the king passed a law against playing it. The law stated, "There is great noise. . . caused by hustling over large balls from which many evils may arise." Anyone caught playing soccer at that time was imprisoned. Two hundred years later, Queen Elizabeth I still had people put in jail for playing this "vulgar" sport.

Despite these laws, soccer grew more popular. In 1681 it became an official sport in England. By the 1800s, people throughout the country played soccer. By the eighteenth century, upper-class boys at private schools played it. Its popularity grew among all English people.

At a meeting held in an English school in 1843, the first rules were suggested. In 1863 the heads of English soccer teams met in London to agree on some official rules. They organized an English football association. By 1871 all of the English clubs were following these rules. Today all soccer teams play by them.

Soccer is called "football" everywhere but in the United States. The rules are simple. There are 11 players on a side. Soccer is played on a field, called a *pitch,* 75 yards wide by 120 yards long. At each end of the pitch is an 8-yards-by-8-feet net—the goal. The object of the game is to get the ball into the opponent's goal. A goalie blocks the goal to prevent the ball from going in. Goalies may catch the ball with their hands. No other players, though, may touch the ball with their hands. Players may propel the ball with their legs or their heads. They may control the ball with any part of the body except their hands. A *hand ball* receives an automatic penalty.

Soccer is by far the world's most popular sport. Every four years, nearly every nation in the world competes in the World Cup. Tens of billions of soccer fans from around the world watch the World Cup on television.

Reading Time _____

Recalling Facts

1. In the 1300s, playing soccer was against the law because it was
   - ❑ a. considered noisy and dangerous.
   - ❑ b. played by poor working people.
   - ❑ c. played with a severed head.

2. Before the mid-1800s, the game of soccer differed from place to place in England, because
   - ❑ a. there were very few soccer teams.
   - ❑ b. it was still against the law to play soccer.
   - ❑ c. there were no official rules of the game.

3. A soccer team scores a point when
   - ❑ a. the goalie catches the ball.
   - ❑ b. it gets the ball into the opponent's net.
   - ❑ c. the other team handles the ball.

4. A soccer player is penalized when he or she
   - ❑ a. hits the ball into the goal with his or her head.
   - ❑ b. kicks the ball out of bounds.
   - ❑ c. touches the ball with his or her hands.

5. The World Cup is played by
   - ❑ a. college teams.
   - ❑ b. teams from many countries.
   - ❑ c. only teams belonging to the English Football Association.

Understanding Ideas

6. One can conclude that
   - ❑ a. Queen Elizabeth I enjoyed watching soccer.
   - ❑ b. today's rules of soccer are at least 100 years old.
   - ❑ c. children in private schools no longer like to play soccer.

7. One can infer from the passage that, throughout the ages,
   - ❑ a. soccer's popularity could not be suppressed.
   - ❑ b. people in most of the world have lost interest in soccer.
   - ❑ c. soccer has been enjoyed mostly by those in the upper class.

8. Which of the following sentences best expresses the main idea?
   - ❑ a. Popular sports that began in England include soccer.
   - ❑ b. The English played soccer during the reign of King Edward I.
   - ❑ c. Soccer, which began in England, was once outlawed but later became popular there and throughout the world.

9. Official rules for soccer were most likely established because
   - ❑ a. disputes arose between teams about how to play the game.
   - ❑ b. some teams cheated.
   - ❑ c. without rules the game was too noisy and violent.

10. The author of this passage would most likely agree that
    - ❑ a. American football should be more popular than soccer.
    - ❑ b. soccer is a popular game.
    - ❑ c. the rules of soccer are unfair.

The Oneidas: First American Soccer Team

Historians claim that, by the 1800s, soccer was being played at colleges in the United States. At first, teams from different schools played by different rules. The college game was also violent. One observer compared it to a bullfight. Many school officials thought that soccer was too rough. For a while, people lost interest in it.

Yet soccer was not dead, just dormant. It quietly became popular again in the New England states. Every fall boys could be seen kicking balls across fields and into nets. Local teams played each other on Saturday afternoons.

By 1862 some players from Boston had formed the Oneida soccer team. This was the first organized team in the United States. Its leader was Gerritt Miller, a great athlete and natural leader. The Oneidas played other teams on the grassy Boston Common. On November 7, 1863, they beat another team by a score of 12–0. The Boston press hailed the team's win. Soccer became even more popular. In the years that followed, the Oneidas won every game they played.

There is some question about just what game the team played. Some people say that it was more like American football than English soccer. It is likely, however, that some players, perhaps Miller, had traveled to England and learned the game there.

1. **Recognizing Words in Context**

   Find the word *dormant* in the passage. One definition below is closest to the meaning of that word. One definition has the opposite or nearly the opposite meaning. The remaining definition has a completely different meaning. Label the definitions C for *closest*, O for *opposite or nearly opposite*, and D for *different*.

   _____ a. sleeping

   _____ b. illegal

   _____ c. active

2. **Distinguishing Fact from Opinion**

   Two of the statements below present *facts*, which can be proved. The other statement is an *opinion*, which expresses someone's thoughts or beliefs. Label the statements F for *fact* and O for *opinion*.

   _____ a. The Oneidas played soccer in Boston.

   _____ b. Teams played each other on Saturday afternoons.

   _____ c. The game of soccer is much too violent for young children to play.

3. Keeping Events in Order

Number the statements below 1, 2, and 3 to show the order in which the events took place.

_____ a. Boston players formed the Oneidas soccer team.

_____ b. The Oneidas won a soccer game by a score of 12–0.

_____ c. Soccer was played only at colleges.

4. Making Correct Inferences

Two of the statements below are correct *inferences*, or reasonable guesses. They are based on information in the passage. The other statement is an incorrect, or faulty, inference. Label the statements C for *correct* inference and F for *faulty* inference.

_____ a. The Oneidas liked to play violently to injure opposing players.

_____ b. Boys playing soccer in the 1800s did not follow official rules.

_____ c. Newspaper coverage of the Oneidas' victories led more people to like soccer.

5. Understanding Main Ideas

One of the statements below expresses the main idea of the passage. One statement is too general, or too broad. The other explains only part of the passage; it is too narrow. Label the statements M for *main idea*, B for *too broad*, and N for *too narrow*.

_____ a. Sports, such as soccer and football, are popular in many parts of the world.

_____ b. The Oneidas soccer team helped to popularize soccer in the United States.

_____ c. Soccer was popular in American colleges in the 1800s.

Correct Answers, Part A _____

Correct Answers, Part B _____

Total Correct Answers _____

Life in the Stone Age

The Stone Age is named for the stone tools used by early human beings of this era. During the late Stone Age, the first true human beings appeared. They were called *Homo sapiens*. One group—the Neandertals (sometimes spelled *Neanderthals*)—thrived in Europe between about 250,000 and 30,000 years ago.

The Neandertals' brains were about the same size as those of modern human beings. However, their skulls were more sloping. Neandertals were equipped to survive a hard life and withstand cold. These people were not dim-witted brutes. They had a somewhat complex, organized way of life.

Neandertals have been called "cave dwellers." Most did live in caves during the winter, yet they were nomadic as well. They traveled in pursuit of game. In summer they built huts or tents out of mammoth bones or wood covered with animal skins.

These people lived in groups of 30 to 50. Their average life span was 40 years. As a result, there were many children in each group. Neandertal children grew up quickly. They could fend for themselves at an early age.

Neandertals were hunter-gatherers. The women gathered plant food. They used stone digging tools to dig up roots and stone sickles to cut grain. The men hunted animals for meat. They used a variety of stone blades and stone spear points to kill game. These stone blades were often attached to wooden handles. Neandertals could control fire. They used it to cook food and to keep warm.

The people made a variety of stone tools. They used axes to chop down trees for wood, blades to cut meat, and scrapers to remove flesh from animal hides. Neandertals made clothing from animal skins. They softened the tough hide by chewing it. This practice wore down their teeth quickly.

The men hunted at close range. Hunting was therefore very dangerous. Injuries were common. There is evidence that Neandertals cared for and fed injured group members. When a group member died, he or she was buried, sometimes with flowers. Stone markers were placed over some graves. This suggests that Neandertals may have practiced rituals connected with a belief in an afterlife.

In 1996 a flute was found at a Neandertal site. Other sites have yielded what may be jewelry—polished bones made into pendants or with zigzag patterns scratched on them. This evidence shows that Neandertals, like modern people, probably created music and art.

Reading Time _____

Recalling Facts

1. Neandertals lived in Europe
   - ❏ a. 10,000 years ago.
   - ❏ b. between 250,000 and 30,000 years ago.
   - ❏ c. millions of years ago.

2. Hunting was dangerous for Neandertals primarily because
   - ❏ a. they had to travel far to find animals.
   - ❏ b. all animals were very large.
   - ❏ c. they killed at close range.

3. Neandertals wore down their teeth quickly by
   - ❏ a. eating raw meat.
   - ❏ b. chewing hide to soften it.
   - ❏ c. making tools out of stone.

4. There were more children than adults in Neandertal groups because
   - ❏ a. children were valuable as workers.
   - ❏ b. adults left the group for long periods of time.
   - ❏ c. adults died at an early age.

5. Neandertals and modern human beings are different in that Neandertals
   - ❏ a. hunted animals.
   - ❏ b. had more sloping skulls.
   - ❏ c. used animal skins for clothing.

Understanding Ideas

6. From the passage, one can infer that most Neandertal children
   - ❏ a. were not cared for by adults.
   - ❏ b. died before they reached adulthood.
   - ❏ c. learned survival skills from their parents.

7. What information in the passage suggests that Neandertals may have believed in an afterlife?
   - ❏ a. Neandertals made and wore jewelry.
   - ❏ b. Neandertals buried their dead with care.
   - ❏ c. Neandertals followed rituals when killing game.

8. Neandertals attached blades to wooden handles in order to
   - ❏ a. beat animals down.
   - ❏ b. protect themselves from charging animals.
   - ❏ c. make tools easier to use.

9. From the way they treated injured group members, one can infer that Neandertals were often
   - ❏ a. brutal.
   - ❏ b. uncaring.
   - ❏ c. kind.

10. According to the description of Neandertal life in the passage, the author would probably agree with which of the following statements?
    - ❏ a. Neandertal and modern people have much in common.
    - ❏ b. Neandertals were not very intelligent.
    - ❏ c. Neandertals, in most aspects, were unlike modern human beings.

50

Stone Age tools may look crude today, yet they were finely crafted. They helped Neandertals survive for thousands of years. Some of these tools were large, heavy stones. They were used as clubs and other blunt instruments. Most other tools were *knapped*—chipped and shaped for specific uses.

Neandertals learned to identify rocks that would produce the best tools. They studied the fault lines in a rock to figure out how it would break. They used large hammer stones to knap rocks. The pieces that came off the rock would then be shaped. Often they would put a rock piece on an *anvil,* a large, hard rock. Then they would strike the piece with stones to shape it. Neandertals made axes, daggers, spearheads, and chisels. They made choppers for smashing bones to reach the tasty marrow. They also made sharp points, "knife" blades to cut flesh, needlelike piercers, and scrapers for cleaning hides. Many Neandertal cutting tools were chipped around the rim. This made their edges very sharp.

Neandertals also knew how to fashion wood. Spearheads, axes, blades, and other stone tools were often bound—or *hafted*—to wooden handles. Usually animal gut was used to attach the tool to the handle. Axes were used to cut down trees. Some Neandertal homes were of wood covered with hide or plant material.

1. **Recognizing Words in Context**

   Find the word *knap* in the passage. One definition below is closest to the meaning of that word. One definition has the opposite or nearly the opposite meaning. The remaining definition has a completely different meaning. Label the definitions C for *closest,* O for *opposite or nearly opposite,* and D for *different.*

   _____ a. bind or fit into

   _____ b. sleep or rest

   _____ c. shape by chipping

2. **Distinguishing Fact from Opinion**

   Two of the statements below present *facts,* which can be proved. The other statement is an *opinion,* which expresses someone's thoughts or beliefs. Label the statements F for *fact* and O for *opinion.*

   _____ a. Neandertals often shaped rocks on anvils.

   _____ b. Neandertals' stone tools were cruder than any other early human beings' tools.

   _____ c. Neandertal tools had sharp edges.

3. Keeping Events in Order

Number the statements below 1, 2, and 3 to show the order in which the events took place.

_____ a. A rock suitable for knapping was identified.

_____ b. The piece was shaped on an anvil.

_____ c. The rock was broken with a hammer stone.

4. Making Correct Inferences

Two of the statements below are correct *inferences,* or reasonable guesses. They are based on information in the passage. The other statement is an incorrect, or faulty, inference. Label the statements C for *correct* inference and F for *faulty* inference.

_____ a. Neandertals liked to eat the marrow from animals' bones.

_____ b. Neandertals used the same tools for tens of thousands of years.

_____ c. Neandertals knew how to build their own shelters.

5. Understanding Main Ideas

One of the statements below expresses the main idea of the passage. One statement is too general, or too broad. The other explains only part of the passage; it is too narrow. Label the statements M for *main idea,* B for *too broad,* and N for *too narrow.*

_____ a. Neandertals made stone tools and weapons, cared for one another, and probably created music and art.

_____ b. Neandertals were experts at identifying rocks that would break easily.

_____ c. Early human beings, such as the Neandertals, developed many survival skills.

Correct Answers, Part A _____

Correct Answers, Part B _____

Total Correct Answers _____

Space Technology and Geography

Geography is the study of Earth and its climates. Scientists use it to study global warming and track the weather. Governments use it to learn where people live and work and to plan what to do with the land. It is now easier than ever to use geography because of a science called space technology.

The United States launched its first satellite in 1958. Some space missions that followed were geographical studies. In fact, earth science is a big part of the work of the National Aeronautics and Space Administration (NASA).

Astronauts looked out of the space shuttle. They decided to take photographs of Earth from their vantage point. Over the years, picture quality improved. Shuttle photography now shows land features, such as rivers. It can even show the streets of large cities. Photos of the same places at different times show how the land is changing.

NASA does not use just photographs, though. In 1958 it launched TIROS (the Television Infrared Observation Satellite). This first use of a satellite to study Earth was effective in giving weather forecasts. It led to the creation of new space tools to use in geography.

The Landsat Program began in 1972. This satellite sent detailed views of Earth from space. The pictures were so precise that scientists could count the number and kinds of crops in a field. Landsat showed where Earth's surface had faults along which earthquakes might occur. This information helped in the planning of new cities and factories. Landsat also made discoveries. In Antarctica it located ranges of unknown mountains. It pinpointed small lakes in Virginia that were not on maps. Landsat, now more advanced, still flies today.

Another space tool is Earth Observing-1 (EO-1). This spacecraft flies right behind Landsat. It takes pictures of the same sites. The two sets of pictures, viewed together, show how cities grow and how other places, such as rain forests, shrink over time. This helps scientists learn how people affect geography.

One of the newest space tools is the Geographical Information Systems (GIS). GIS is computer software. It obtains data from satellites that helps scientists to study Earth. GIS has allowed scientists to note such changes as erosion on the coast of Israel. GIS is different from earlier space tools. Businesses, schools, and even average people—not just the government— can use it to show them how changes in the planet might affect them.

Reading Time _____

Recalling Facts

1. The U.S. satellite program began in
   - ❑ a. 1972.
   - ❑ b. 1958.
   - ❑ c. 1999.

2. Governments study geography to
   - ❑ a. improve business plans.
   - ❑ b. plan land use.
   - ❑ c. set laws.

3. TIROS was most successful in
   - ❑ a. taking photos of Earth.
   - ❑ b. making weather predictions.
   - ❑ c. launching other satellites.

4. Landsat was able to
   - ❑ a. take pictures of other planets.
   - ❑ b. track weather systems.
   - ❑ c. find new mountains in Antarctica.

5. GIS is a unique space tool in that it
   - ❑ a. can be used by average people.
   - ❑ b. is operated by the largest satellite.
   - ❑ c. was the first satellite in orbit.

Understanding Ideas

6. From the passage, one can infer that recent U.S. satellites are
   - ❑ a. similar to previous ones.
   - ❑ b. limited in their usefulness.
   - ❑ c. more advanced.

7. The best example of how space tools can help businesses select locations is
   - ❑ a. showing how rain forests are shrinking.
   - ❑ b. showing fault lines where earthquakes could happen.
   - ❑ c. showing the growth pattern of city streets.

8. EO-1 takes photographs of the same places as Landsat
   - ❑ a. so that scientists can compare the two sets of pictures to see changes in Earth.
   - ❑ b. because EO-1 is practicing for future photography missions.
   - ❑ c. because Landsat is out of date and needs back-up data.

9. The fact that Landsat discovered new geographical features suggests that
   - ❑ a. those features have only recently developed.
   - ❑ b. the satellite made an error.
   - ❑ c. satellite images capture more detail than older map-making methods did.

10. Which of the following statements best describes the main idea?
   - ❑ a. New space technology tools help geographers in numerous fields.
   - ❑ b. Space technology has made many advances since 1958.
   - ❑ c. GIS makes it possible for everyone to use geography every day.

One of the most exciting space tools is the Global Positioning System (GPS). It pinpoints the location of a person or a thing anywhere on Earth. It is run by the United States Department of Defense.

The GPS is made up of 24 satellites. They orbit Earth once every 12 hours at an altitude of 11,000 nautical miles. Each satellite emits timed signals. The receiver receives three signals, one from each of three satellites. One is for latitude, one for longitude, and one for altitude. The receiver finds out how long it takes for the signals to come in. It then uses this information in computing location.

GPS has many uses. It can tell ships where they are at sea. It helps planes to land in poor weather when pilots cannot see clearly. Experts use it to survey the Earth.

There are two types of GPS. One is for the government and military. One is for other people. The government has Precise Positioning System (PPS). Civilians use Standard Position Service (SPS). PPS is better, but SPS still does a great job. It is accurate to within 100 meters.

GPS is changing how people drive, hike, and make maps. A consumer can buy a GPS receiver for a few hundred dollars. GPS can be found inside cell phones, cars, and watches.

1. **Recognizing Words in Context**

Find the word *consumer* in the passage. One definition below is closest to the meaning of that word. One definition has the opposite or nearly the opposite meaning. The remaining definition has a completely different meaning. Label the definitions C for *closest,* O for *opposite or nearly opposite,* and D for *different.*

_____ a. seller

_____ b. buyer

_____ c. pilot

2. **Distinguishing Fact from Opinion**

Two of the statements below present *facts,* which can be proved. The other statement is an *opinion,* which expresses someone's thoughts or beliefs. Label the statements F for *fact* and O for *opinion.*

_____ a. GPS uses 24 orbiting satellites.

_____ b. The GPS receiver receives signals of three kinds.

_____ c. Using GPS is better than using a map on paper.

3. Keeping Events in Order

Number the statements below 1, 2, and 3 to show the order in which the events took place.

_____ a. The Department of Defense launched 24 satellites.

_____ b. Three satellites sent signals to a receiver on Earth.

_____ c. A receiver adjusted the time difference.

4. Making Correct Inferences

Two of the statements below are correct *inferences*, or reasonable guesses. They are based on information in the passage. The other statement is an incorrect, or faulty, inference. Label the statements C for *correct* inference and F for *faulty* inference.

_____ a. The government does not want ordinary citizens to use GPS technology.

_____ b. GPS can make it easier to find one's destination when driving in a car.

_____ c. GPS was originally intended to have military uses.

5. Understanding Main Ideas

One of the statements below expresses the main idea of the passage. One statement is too general, or too broad. The other explains only part of the passage; it is too narrow. Label the statements M for *main idea*, B for *too broad*, and N for *too narrow*.

_____ a. GPS is being used by ordinary people when they drive.

_____ b. GPS is a satellite-based geographic tool that has many uses.

_____ c. Satellites in space send signals to Earth.

Correct Answers, Part A _____

Correct Answers, Part B _____

Total Correct Answers _____

Creoles and Cajuns in Louisiana

Creoles and Cajuns are two groups of people living in Louisiana. Both groups settled there long ago. Both also have ancestors who came from France. Each group has as interesting a history as do the words *Creole* and *Cajun*.

The English word *Creole* comes from three other languages: French, Spanish, and Portuguese. To a person from one of these countries, a Creole is a European citizen born in the colonies in America. In Louisiana, on the other hand, a Creole is a person born in that state. Creole families were the first to settle in the region. Most of the early Creole settlers were from the French upper classes. Some wanted to be part of the ruling class in their new land. Since the Civil War, American society has changed. Today the largest Creole community is found in southeastern Louisiana. Many Creoles live in New Orleans.

The word *Cajun* comes from the word *Acadian*. This group also came from France. They settled in eastern Canada. They named the settlement Acadia. The Acadians had been peasants in France. In their new home, they became farmers. In 1755 some Acadians left their homeland when the British defeated the French in Canada. Some, lured by the French culture in Louisiana, moved there. Most Cajuns live in the southwestern part of the state. At first, they did not get along well with the Creoles. With time, however, some married into the elite Creole society.

Words, too, change over time. The term *Creole* has taken on many meanings. The result can be confusing. In the past, some people called themselves Creoles to show that they were not Cajuns. Today the meaning of the word is broader. It is often used to describe many things that are Cajun. It also describes things that are purely Creole.

Both cultures, like American culture in general, are a mixture of influences. Cajun French includes African and English words, for example. Creole music is called Zydeco. It combines French folk music with African rhythms. The words of the songs are often in Creole French. Creole cooking uses peppers from Mexico. It also uses herbs that grow wild in Louisiana. Gumbo, a thick soup, is made with tomatoes, onions, and a vegetable called okra. It also contains chicken and sausage. Many people think that the name of the dish comes from an African word, *gambo,* which means "okra."

Reading Time _____

Recalling Facts

1. Creoles and Cajuns are
   - ❑ a. different groups that came from Mexico.
   - ❑ b. different French-speaking groups that settled in Louisiana.
   - ❑ c. groups in the United States that continue to speak Spanish.

2. The English word *Creole*
   - ❑ a. was coined by people living in the United States.
   - ❑ b. describes people who have just moved to Louisiana.
   - ❑ c. comes from the French, Spanish, and Portuguese languages.

3. The word *Cajun*
   - ❑ a. comes from the word *Acadian*.
   - ❑ b. is a name given to Africans living in Louisiana.
   - ❑ c. is taken from the Portuguese language.

4. Creole life in Louisiana is
   - ❑ a. very different from life elsewhere in the United States.
   - ❑ b. a mixture of many influences.
   - ❑ c. known for its very plain food.

5. Gumbo is a
   - ❑ a. nickname for the southwestern part of Louisiana.
   - ❑ b. thick soup made with okra, tomatoes, chicken, and sausage.
   - ❑ c. kind of French folk music.

Understanding Ideas

6. One can conclude that
   - ❑ a. the meaning of a word never changes.
   - ❑ b. at any time the meaning of a word is always clear.
   - ❑ c. the meanings of words may change over time.

7. From the passage, one can infer that immigrants of the same ethnic origin
   - ❑ a. may bring different experiences and values to their new home.
   - ❑ b. always share the same language and values.
   - ❑ c. always band together in their new homeland.

8. The mixture of influence in Creole and Cajun cultures shows that people
   - ❑ a. adhere strictly to their own traditions.
   - ❑ b. tend to ignore other cultures.
   - ❑ c. adopt ideas from other cultures.

9. If one would like to experience the Creole culture, one should
   - ❑ a. visit southern Louisiana.
   - ❑ b. plan a visit to Canada.
   - ❑ c. travel anywhere in the South.

10. Which of the following sentences best explains what the passage is about?
    - ❑ a. The words *Cajun* and *Creole* have been used differently over time.
    - ❑ b. Both Creoles and Cajuns in Louisiana have roots in French culture and language but are distinct groups.
    - ❑ c. The United States is a mixture of many influences, including languages and cultures from Europe and Africa.

Zydeco Music: Creole Gumbo

Zydeco music is part of Creole life. It became popular in the 1940s. Most people find it hard not to dance when they hear its beat. The main instrument in a zydeco band is the accordion. Drums, a fiddle, a bass guitar, and the washboard are often part of zydeco music.

The washboard is a metal board with ridges. Years ago it was used on washing day for scrubbing clothes. Zydeco musicians call it by the French word *frottoir* (frōtwär). Today, a *frottoir* has straps. It is worn over a person's chest, like a vest. Players make sounds by running scrapers across its grooved surface. Scrapers can be anything made of metal, such as thimbles or spoons.

Zydeco combines different kinds of musical influences. Some of the rhythms come from Africa. The guitar is a Spanish instrument. Many French settlers brought violins with them. The accordion was invented in the 1800s in Austria. Many Zydeco songs are sung in the Creole form of French. The high pitch of the singing can sound like mournful crying, or keening. Some people say that this style comes from the chants of Native Americans.

There are many styles of zydeco, including a modern one. It sounds a bit like hip-hop music. Zydeco is a "musical gumbo." It is full of different flavors, just like the tasty Creole soup.

1. Recognizing Words in Context

Find the word *keening* in the passage. One definition below is closest to the meaning of that word. One definition has the opposite or nearly the opposite meaning. The remaining definition has a completely different meaning. Label the definitions C for *closest*, O for *opposite or nearly opposite*, and D for *different*.

_____ a. whispering

_____ b. stomping

_____ c. wailing

2. Distinguishing Fact from Opinion

Two of the statements below present *facts*, which can be proved. The other statement is an *opinion*, which expresses someone's thoughts or beliefs. Label the statements F for *fact* and O for *opinion*.

_____ a. Some zydeco musicians play on a washboard called a *frottoir*.

_____ b. Zydeco music makes people want to dance.

_____ c. The main instrument in a zydeco band is the accordion.

3. Keeping Events in Order

Number the statements below 1, 2, and 3 to show the order in which the events took place.

_____ a. The accordion was invented in Austria.

_____ b. Zydeco came to sound a bit like hip-hop music.

_____ c. Zydeco music became part of Creole life.

4. Making Correct Inferences

Two of the statements below are correct *inferences,* or reasonable guesses. They are based on information in the passage. The other statement is an incorrect, or faulty, inference. Label the statements C for *correct* inference and F for *faulty* inference.

_____ a. Musicians can make instruments from everyday objects.

_____ b. The word *gumbo* (a kind of soup) can also be used to mean "mixture."

_____ c. Zydeco music will not change in the future.

5. Understanding Main Ideas

One of the statements below expresses the main idea of the passage. One statement is too general, or too broad. The other explains only part of the passage; it is too narrow. Label the statements M for *main idea,* B for *too broad,* and N for *too narrow.*

_____ a. Zydeco is rhythmic Creole music that combines instruments and musical elements from many cultures.

_____ b. A *frottoir* is played by running metal scrapers over its grooved surface.

_____ c. Zydeco is one example of the many influences of Creole culture.

Correct Answers, Part A _____

Correct Answers, Part B _____

Total Correct Answers _____

Historical fiction is a key part of many social studies classes. Good historical fiction blends facts with storytelling skill. These stories take place in the past. The main characters are almost always fictional. These characters are usually involved in a serious conflict. They must overcome huge odds. Often their lives are in danger. Some of the best-known historical-fiction writers are Avi, Dolores Johnson, and Lois Lowry.

Historical novels have the potential to capture students' interest in history. Historical facts are included as part of the stories, helping to make the past an interesting place for students to visit. Dramatic techniques such as plot, dialogue, and conflict help the reader to enjoy the magic of a story. Through reading about a character, the student relates to him or her. This helps the reader to understand the time and place better.

Historical fiction relies on factual details to make the story seem real, so accuracy is vital in this genre. Authors spend many hours researching the places and time periods for their books. Through reading historical fiction, students can learn about clothing, food, and tools from a certain time in history. This background provides a good framework for considering ways of life in other times. Students can also learn about speech patterns and social customs from historical novels. This knowledge helps them to recognize how a culture changes over time.

Historical fiction also helps connect the past to contemporary daily life. Students can regard the characters from history almost as real people. They can make important links between the past and their own lives.

Number the Stars, by Lois Lowry, is a good example of historical fiction. This story takes place during World War II. It relates how a 10-year-old girl, with her family, helps to smuggle a young girl out of Nazi-occupied Denmark. The book features a made-up character in a real setting. True details about the war and life during the 1940s appear.

Another good example is *Now Let Me Fly: The Story of a Slave Family* by Dolores Johnson. It tells the story of Minna, a young African girl. She is sold to a slave trader and brought to America. Minna is a made-up character whose story is set in the eighteenth century. The story gives the reader an accurate picture of what life was like for some enslaved African Americans of that time.

Reading Time _____

Recalling Facts

1. Historical fiction blends historical facts with
   - ❑ a. architectural drawings.
   - ❑ b. musical scores.
   - ❑ c. storytelling skill.

2. Historical novels are set in
   - ❑ a. the past.
   - ❑ b. current times.
   - ❑ c. the future.

3. A key component of historical fiction is
   - ❑ a. illustrations.
   - ❑ b. factual details.
   - ❑ c. complicated plots.

4. One dramatic technique used in historical fiction is
   - ❑ a. typesetting.
   - ❑ b. dialogue.
   - ❑ c. charts.

5. Historical fiction is probably used most often in
   - ❑ a. science classes.
   - ❑ b. math classes.
   - ❑ c. social studies classes.

Understanding Ideas

6. One can conclude from the passage that authors of historical fiction
   - ❑ a. enjoy research.
   - ❑ b. have traveled extensively.
   - ❑ c. know many languages.

7. It is likely that teachers use historical fiction in their classes because
   - ❑ a. historical novels are less expensive than textbooks.
   - ❑ b. nonfiction books do not present facts as accurately as historical novels do.
   - ❑ c. it helps them to bring history "to life" for students.

8. Compared with science fiction, historical fiction
   - ❑ a. has more female characters.
   - ❑ b. takes place in a specific time in history.
   - ❑ c. deals with problems of adolescents.

9. One can conclude from the passage that
   - ❑ a. all teachers use historical novels in their classes.
   - ❑ b. good historical fiction presents an accurate view of a time period.
   - ❑ c. the best young-adult books are historical fiction.

10. Which of the following best presents the author's view of historical fiction?
   - ❑ a. Historical fiction is a helpful addition to a social studies curriculum.
   - ❑ b. Historical fiction will soon replace traditional textbooks.
   - ❑ c. Reading historical fiction is vital to understanding history.

Avi Wortis, known simply as Avi, writes historical fiction. He decided to be a writer when he was a senior in high school. This was quite a decision because he did not write well in school. He has a condition called *dysgraphia,* a writing impairment. The problem causes people to switch letters in, and misspell, words. Avi has always enjoyed reading. He read many types of books as a child. Avi believes that reading is the most important activity for a person who wants to be a writer.

Avi also believes that strong characters make strong stories. He creates characters that can help to bring his ideas to life. His books often relate to questions about life. Writing stories lets him explore many sides of an issue. His favorite part of the writing process is the revision. For him the hardest part is writing the first draft.

Avi's first book was published in 1970. He has since written more than 45 books. Most of them are for young-adult readers. He writes in a wide range of genres—comedies, fantasies, short stories, and ghost stories. *Fighting Ground,* which was published in 1984, is an example of one of Avi's historical novels. The fascinating story takes place during the American Revolutionary War.

1. **Recognizing Words in Context**

    Find the word *impairment* in the passage. One definition below is closest to the meaning of that word. One definition has the opposite or nearly the opposite meaning. The remaining definition has a completely different meaning. Label the definitions C for *closest,* O for *opposite or nearly opposite,* and D for *different.*

    _____ a. remedy

    _____ b. imperfection

    _____ c. determination

2. **Distinguishing Fact from Opinion**

    Two of the statements below present *facts,* which can be proved. The other statement is an *opinion,* which expresses someone's thoughts or beliefs. Label the statements F for *fact* and O for *opinion.*

    _____ a. The hardest part of writing is the creation of the first draft.

    _____ b. Avi writes in a wide range of genres.

    _____ c. Avi has a condition called dysgraphia.

3. Keeping Events in Order

Number the statements below 1, 2, and 3 to show the order in which the events took place.

_____ a. Avi published his first book.

_____ b. Avi read many kinds of books to help him learn to be a writer.

_____ c. Avi published *Fighting Ground.*

4. Making Correct Inferences

Two of the statements below are correct *inferences,* or reasonable guesses. They are based on information in the passage. The other statement is an incorrect, or faulty, inference. Label the statements C for *correct* inference and F for *faulty* inference.

_____ a. Writing stories can help someone to understand complex issues in that person's own life.

_____ b. People who have dysgraphia always become successful writers.

_____ c. Writing stories can help a person see different sides of an issue.

5. Understanding Main Ideas

One of the statements below expresses the main idea of the passage. One statement is too general, or too broad. The other explains only part of the passage; it is too narrow. Label the statements M for *main idea*, B for *too broad,* and N for *too narrow.*

_____ a. *Fighting Ground* is a historical novel that Avi wrote.

_____ b. Writers of young-adult fiction work hard to succeed.

_____ c. Avi has had a diverse writing career, working in many genres.

Correct Answers, Part A _____

Correct Answers, Part B _____

Total Correct Answers _____

The Storming of the Bastille

The Bastille was an infamous building in France. King Charles V built it in 1371 as a castle. Later this stronghold was used as a prison. After 1670 it became a jail for people of wealth and high rank who had fallen out of favor with the king. For more than a century, it symbolized the ruthless power of the king and the wealthy. The structure was a fortress whose walls were 10 feet thick. It was surrounded by a moat. Cannons pointed down from its highest towers.

In the late 1780s, France had a very rigid, unfair social structure. The common people were desperately poor and had little or no chance of bettering their position. Meanwhile, the royal family, aristocrats, and church officials were rich. They were also arrogant. They believed that they had the right to live in luxury while the masses suffered.

The times were ripe for revolution. The Enlightenment was sweeping Europe. This philosophy taught that all people had the basic right to life, liberty, and equality. Because of these beliefs, the American colonies had revolted against British rule. The colonists won their freedom. The French people acted on these same beliefs. In 1789 the French Revolution began with the storming of the Bastille.

In July of 1789, citizens in Paris were alarmed. A rumor had spread that troops were being sent to disband the people's National Assembly. An angry mob wanted to stop them. On July 14, a group of citizens marched through Paris. Their target was the Bastille—the hated symbol of power and injustice. The crowd shouted, "Down with the Bastille." They attracted more followers as they swept through the city. When they reached the Bastille, some guards joined them. They managed to cut the chains on a drawbridge, which was then lowered over the moat. The mob poured into the prison. Despite some loss of life, the citizens fought bravely. They battled to gain access to the interior of the jail. After an intense battle, the prison guards surrendered. The crowd ran through the jail, releasing all of its prisoners.

The Bastille contained a supply of arms. The victorious citizens seized these weapons. The weapons would prove useful in fighting the revolution they had just begun.

According to legend, when King Louis XVI heard that Parisians had stormed the Bastille, he exclaimed, "This is a revolt." A duke replied, "No, sire, it is a revolution!"

Reading Time _____

Recalling Facts

1. Some time after it was built, the Bastille was used as a
   - ❏ a. prison.
   - ❏ b. palace.
   - ❏ c. concert hall.

2. The Enlightenment promoted a philosophy that taught that all people
   - ❏ a. have a right to liberty.
   - ❏ b. should have access to wealth.
   - ❏ c. should overthrow their government.

3. For the people of France, the Bastille was a symbol of
   - ❏ a. the church.
   - ❏ b. injustice.
   - ❏ c. foreign power.

4. The citizens of Paris were able to enter the Bastille after they
   - ❏ a. killed all of the guards.
   - ❏ b. stole all of the cannons.
   - ❏ c. cut the chains on the drawbridge.

5. The citizens of Paris were aided in their attack on the Bastille by
   - ❏ a. guards who joined their cause.
   - ❏ b. the royal family.
   - ❏ c. Enlightenment philosophers.

Understanding Ideas

6. Compared with the royal family and the aristocrats, the common people of France at this time were
   - ❏ a. content with their lives.
   - ❏ b. extremely poor.
   - ❏ c. philosophical about life.

7. The Enlightenment is believed to have been one cause of the French Revolution because it taught that
   - ❏ a. wealth was an evil.
   - ❏ b. kings should be elected to office.
   - ❏ c. all people deserve liberty and justice.

8. From the king's comment about the storming of the Bastille, "This is a revolt," one can infer that he
   - ❏ a. had little understanding of the people's hardship and anger.
   - ❏ b. was not prepared to call on troops to fight the people.
   - ❏ c. sympathized with the angry mob.

9. One can conclude from the passage that the American Revolution
   - ❏ a. was fought against the king of France.
   - ❏ b. helped to inspire the French to rebel.
   - ❏ c. led to the creation of the National Assembly.

10. The author would most likely agree that the French citizens
    - ❏ a. were right to fight for their liberty.
    - ❏ b. should have had more respect for the king.
    - ❏ c. should not have battled the guards to storm the Bastille.

14   B   Bastille Day

Bastille Day is celebrated as a national holiday in France on July 14. On this day, as with the United States' Independence Day, the people celebrate their liberty and freedom. The French honor the storming of the Bastille in 1789, the event that sparked the French Revolution.

Bastille Day festivities usually start on July 13. On that night, towns and cities all over France hold traditional firemen's balls. All are welcome. People dance, sing, drink, and have fun far into the night.

The next morning, official Bastille Day events begin. In Paris there is a military parade down the wide avenue the *Champs-Elysée*. Later the city's many parks are open to citizens. The people usually celebrate by having picnics. They eat fine French food, quaff glasses of wine, or drink champagne in celebration.

As night falls over Paris, thousands of people gather near the famous Eiffel Tower. Fireworks light up the night sky. Sometimes there are also light shows of colorful laser beams. The streets in this part of Paris are, of course, closed to all traffic. People party in the streets of central Paris until the early hours of the morning. On Bastille Day, a good time is had by all!

1. **Recognizing Words in Context**

   Find the word *quaff* in the passage. One definition below is closest to the meaning of that word. One definition has the opposite or nearly the opposite meaning. The remaining definition has a completely different meaning. Label the definitions C for *closest,* O for *opposite or nearly opposite,* and D for *different.*

   _____ a. drink

   _____ b. abstain

   _____ c. sell

2. **Distinguishing Fact from Opinion**

   Two of the statements below present *facts,* which can be proved. The other statement is an *opinion,* which expresses someone's thoughts or beliefs. Label the statements F for *fact* and O for *opinion.*

   _____ a. Firemen's balls are a French tradition.

   _____ b. Everyone has a good time on Bastille Day.

   _____ c. Bastille Day begins with a military parade.

3. Keeping Events in Order

Number the statements below 1, 2, and 3 to show the order in which the events take place.

_____ a. Fireworks light up the sky.

_____ b. People go to their local firemen's ball.

_____ c. There are military parades down the *Champs-Elysée.*

4. Making Correct Inferences

Two of the statements below are correct *inferences,* or reasonable guesses. They are based on information in the passage. The other statement is an incorrect, or faulty, inference. Label the statements C for *correct* inference and F for *faulty* inference.

_____ a. Bastille Day celebrations are an important tradition for the French people.

_____ b. Laser light shows and fireworks are popular in France.

_____ c. The French are eager to start a revolution against their government.

5. Understanding Main Ideas

One of the statements below expresses the main idea of the passage. One statement is too general, or too broad. The other explains only part of the passage; it is too narrow. Label the statements M for *main idea,* B for *too broad,* and N for *too narrow.*

_____ a. The French people celebrate Bastille Day with parades and festivities.

_____ b. Firemen's balls are a tradition associated with Bastille Day.

_____ c. People around the world celebrate independence in many ways.

Correct Answers, Part A _____

Correct Answers, Part B _____

Total Correct Answers _____

Franklin Delano Roosevelt and the New Deal

Franklin Delano Roosevelt, who was nicknamed FDR, was born in 1882 into a wealthy family. Roosevelt went to the best schools and colleges. Then he decided to enter politics. In 1910 he was elected to the New York State Senate.

Despite his wealth, FDR understood the needs of the common people. He always fought for their rights. After he served a term as secretary of the Navy, he was elected governor of New York in 1928. At this time, the United States economy was very bad. In 1929 the stock market crashed, and the Great Depression began. Banks and businesses declared bankruptcy. Millions of people lost their jobs and were out of work. Roosevelt began new social programs in the state of New York. He introduced unemployment insurance and pension programs for retirees. He began large public works projects. These projects gave people jobs. His social programs in New York helped many people through the hard times. Through his actions, he showed others how these programs could work. In 1932 FDR ran for president as a Democrat. He won the election in a landslide.

Across the country, the Depression had grown worse. Poverty was widespread. As president, Roosevelt created national programs similar to those he had begun in New York. He called these programs a "New Deal" for America. He got Congress to pass laws that paid relief money to the poor and to farmers. The New Deal included programs that provided jobs for many jobless people. One was the Works Progress Administration. Workers built bridges and roads. They planted trees, and they did other work to help the country. FDR also set up a new type of insurance. This safeguard protected the savings that people kept in banks. As a result, people gained new faith in banks. They began to have more hope for the future. The programs went a long way toward helping to lift the country out of the Depression.

FDR is considered by many one of the greatest presidents ever. He was caring and tireless in his fight to help common people. He was brilliant and full of life, despite the fact that he had contracted polio in 1921, when he was only 39. During much of his presidency, the disease confined him to a wheelchair. His disability, however, was never an obstacle in his fight for a good life for all Americans.

Reading Time _____

Recalling Facts

1. FDR grew up in a family that
   - ❑ a. was unknown.
   - ❑ b. was wealthy.
   - ❑ c. had long periods of unemployment.

2. Just before being elected president, FDR was elected
   - ❑ a. secretary of the Navy.
   - ❑ b. U.S. senator.
   - ❑ c. governor of New York.

3. FDR began his social programs in response to
   - ❑ a. the Great Depression.
   - ❑ b. the New Deal.
   - ❑ c. people's lack of insurance.

4. The U.S. economy collapsed, and the Depression began in
   - ❑ a. 1929.
   - ❑ b. 1910.
   - ❑ c. 1921.

5. FDR was a great leader even though he suffered from
   - ❑ a. poverty.
   - ❑ b. polio.
   - ❑ c. depression.

Understanding Ideas

6. One can infer from the passage that before FDR was president, banks
   - ❑ a. did not insure people's savings.
   - ❑ b. did not pay interest on people's savings.
   - ❑ c. did not accept savings from ordinary people.

7. FDR's public works projects helped relieve poverty because
   - ❑ a. roads helped people get to jobs.
   - ❑ b. they provided jobs for unemployed people.
   - ❑ c. they gave money to the elderly and to farmers.

8. One can conclude from the passage that FDR's main concern was to
   - ❑ a. be reelected as president.
   - ❑ b. make sure that banks stayed in business.
   - ❑ c. lift people out of poverty.

9. The social programs FDR created as governor of New York were similar to those he created as president in that they both
   - ❑ a. involved building roads.
   - ❑ b. improved the U.S. Navy.
   - ❑ c. put people back to work.

10. With which of the following statements would the author of this passage *most* agree?
    - ❑ a. FDR was a good president, but he favored the rich too much.
    - ❑ b. FDR was too rich to understand working people.
    - ❑ c. FDR was an exceptional leader.

WPA Workers

Joblessness and poverty were two severe problems during the Great Depression. President Roosevelt's New Deal helped to ease poverty. It did this by getting people back to work. An integral part of the program was the Works Progress Administration (WPA).

The WPA began in 1935. At that time, when unemployment was still high, the government provided work. A major WPA program was Federal One, a program that gave work to artists.

Each of the program's five parts was devoted to one of the arts. One year after it started, this project employed 40,000 artists.

The fine arts project hired some artists who made sculptures or painted murals on public buildings. Many artists taught free art classes. Photographers were also hired. Some of the best pictures showed the hardships of the times.

The music project employed out-of-work musicians. Some formed bands and orchestras. Some gave free concerts. Others taught music to the public at no charge.

The WPA theater project hired actors and directors to stage plays. Most performances were free. Some famous actors got their start in the WPA.

The writers' project used nearly 7,000 writers. Some wrote guidebooks about each state. Writers interviewed people to learn local history. Some important oral histories, including one on slavery, were written this way.

1. **Recognizing Words in Context**

   Find the word *integral* in the passage. One definition below is closest to the meaning of that word. One definition has the opposite or nearly the opposite meaning. The remaining definition has a completely different meaning. Label the definitions C for *closest*, O for *opposite or nearly opposite*, and D for *different*.

   _____ a. minor

   _____ b. menial

   _____ c. essential

2. **Distinguishing Fact from Opinion**

   Two of the statements below present *facts*, which can be proved. The other statement is an *opinion*, which expresses someone's thoughts or beliefs. Label the statements F for *fact* and O for *opinion*.

   _____ a. The Federal One program gave work to artists.

   _____ b. The theater project put on many free plays.

   _____ c. Artists painted lovely murals on buildings.

3. Keeping Events in Order

Number the statements below 1, 2, and 3 to show the order in which the events took place.

_____ a. Roosevelt was elected president.

_____ b. About 40,000 artists worked for the WPA.

_____ c. The New Deal began.

4. Making Correct Inferences

Two of the statements below are correct *inferences,* or reasonable guesses. They are based on information in the passage. The other statement is an incorrect, or faulty, inference. Label the statements C for *correct* inference and F for *faulty* inference.

_____ a. The WPA wasted money and produced little of value to the United States.

_____ b. The WPA provided opportunities for artists to use their talents to contribute to society.

_____ c. Many Americans received free art lessons.

5. Understanding Main Ideas

One of the statements below expresses the main idea of the passage. One statement is too general, or too broad. The other explains only part of the passage; it is too narrow. Label the statements M for *main idea*, B for *too broad,* and N for *too narrow.*

_____ a. The WPA Federal One program employed thousands of artists and enhanced American culture and art.

_____ b. Throughout history, programs have been set up by governments to help citizens who are suffering economically.

_____ c. The WPA music program enabled many Americans to listen to free concerts.

Correct Answers, Part A _____

Correct Answers, Part B _____

Total Correct Answers _____

Photojournalism: Telling the Story Through Pictures

Photographs are everywhere. They decorate the walls of homes. They are used in stores to promote sales of everything from food to clothes and cars. The news is filled with pictures of fires and floods, special events, and famous faces. Photos record the beauties of nature. They can also bring things close that are far away. Through photos, people can see wild animals, cities in foreign lands, and even the stars in outer space. Photos also tell stories.

Reporting the news through photos is called photojournalism. At times photojournalists tell their stories through a single picture. At other times, they use a group of pictures to tell a story. Each picture is like a chapter in a book. This kind of story is called a photo essay. A photo essay can do more than set down the facts. It can also be a potent force for social change.

Jacob Riis was one of the first photojournalists. He took pictures of parts of New York City where the poor lived. Riis believed that poverty caused crime, and he used photos to help him prove his point. A few years later, the photographs of Lewis Hine shocked the public. The photos showed small children working in factories. Hine's pictures helped bring about laws to protect such children.

Photojournalists try to be present at important events. One early example of this took place after the killing of President Abraham Lincoln in 1865. People wanted to know more about those who were guilty of this crime. Alexander Gardner took pictures of the defendants when they came to trial and were punished.

Hundreds of pictures may have to be taken in order to get one or two really good photos. Making pictures is both a science and an art. It takes science to have the photo come out clearly, rather than blurry or too dark or too light. It takes art to make a photo that has a good design and conveys feeling. Photojournalists make a factual record of what they see. A photo, however, can be both a work of art and a factual record. It can capture an important event as a beautiful or stirring image.

As historical and artistic documents, photos can become more important over time. Today photojournalists still have their pictures appear in newspapers and magazines. They also publish them in books and on the Internet.

Reading Time _____

Recalling Facts

1. A photojournalist is a person
   - ❑ a. who writes news articles.
   - ❑ b. who makes works of art.
   - ❑ c. who reports the news through photographs.

2. A photo essay is
   - ❑ a. a group of photos used to tell a story.
   - ❑ b. a photo that goes with an essay.
   - ❑ c. a book about photography.

3. The photojournalist Jacob Riis took pictures of
   - ❑ a. the parts of New York City where the poor lived.
   - ❑ b. the people put on trial for killing President Lincoln.
   - ❑ c. little children working in factories.

4. To get one good photo, photojournalists
   - ❑ a. take pictures only of beautiful subjects.
   - ❑ b. may have to take hundreds of pictures.
   - ❑ c. ask their subjects to sit very still.

5. Today photojournalists put their pictures
   - ❑ a. only in magazines.
   - ❑ b. in books but not in newspapers.
   - ❑ c. on the Internet as well as in newspapers, magazines, and books.

Understanding Ideas

6. The author believes that
   - ❑ a. the best photojournalists have both technical and artistic skills.
   - ❑ b. all photographs are works of art.
   - ❑ c. Only trained artiists should take photographs for public use.

7. Many people did not know that small children worked in factories
   - ❑ a. because they did not care.
   - ❑ b. until they saw photos like those of Lewis Hine.
   - ❑ c. until after laws were created to protect the children.

8. A photo essay is like a book with chapters in that
   - ❑ a. some books have pictures.
   - ❑ b. writers make up the story as they go along.
   - ❑ c. each picture tells part of the story.

9. When a photojournalist takes photos, he or she probably
   - ❑ a. works slowly so that every picture will be perfect.
   - ❑ b. takes pictures only when something important happens.
   - ❑ c. works quickly to record many aspects of the event so as to have choices from which to select.

10. Which of the following sentences best explains what the article is about?
    - ❑ a. Photojournalists are reporters who tell the news through photographs.
    - ❑ b. Photographs bring things close that are far away.
    - ❑ c. Good photojournalists are also artists.

Dorothea Lange and Her *Migrant Mother*

Dorothea Lange took photos during the Great Depression. Her photos often show a world that is full of pain. The Depression caused many people to lose their jobs and homes. Lange went out into the streets of San Francisco, where she lived, to document the troubles that people faced. Later on, she was hired to take pictures by the U.S. government.

During the Depression, many farmers became migrant workers. They went around the country looking for work picking fruit or weeding fields. In 1936 Lange was on a trip for the government. While she was visiting a camp of migrant pea pickers in California, she met a woman and her children. She took several pictures of them. One of these pictures— *Migrant Mother*—became very famous.

The photo shows the woman seated and resting her chin in her hand. She has a baby on her lap. Two small children lean against her. Their faces are turned away from the camera. Everyone is dirty and wears tattered clothes. Although the woman is young, her face is lined with worry. It seems as though she and her children do not have a home. It is clear that they do not get enough to eat. In 1937 new programs were created to help people such as those in Lange's *Migrant Mother*.

1. Recognizing Words in Context

Find the word *document* in the passage. One definition below is closest to the meaning of that word. One definition has the opposite or nearly the opposite meaning. The remaining definition has a completely different meaning. Label the definitions C for *closest*, O for *opposite or nearly opposite*, and D for *different*.

_____ a. donate

_____ b. record

_____ c. erase

2. Distinguishing Fact from Opinion

Two of the statements below present *facts*, which can be proved. The other statement is an *opinion*, which expresses someone's thoughts or beliefs. Label the statements F for *fact* and O for *opinion*.

_____ a. The woman in *Migrant Mother* looks worried.

_____ b. The Great Depression caused many people to lose their jobs.

_____ c. Dorothea Lange lived in San Francisco.

3. Keeping Events in Order

Number the statements below 1, 2, and 3 to show the order in which the events took place.

_____ a. Dorothea Lange took a photo she called *Migrant Mother.*

_____ b. Dorothea Lange took pictures in San Francisco of people who had lost their jobs.

_____ c. The Great Depression began.

4. Making Correct Inferences

Two of the statements below are correct *inferences,* or reasonable guesses. They are based on information in the passage. The other statement is an incorrect, or faulty, inference. Label the statements C for *correct* inference and F for *faulty* inference.

_____ a. Lange's photograph *Migrant Mother* became a symbol of the hardships of the Great Depression.

_____ b. Photojournalism helped to end the Great Depression.

_____ c. A single photograph can convey much information and emotion.

5. Understanding Main Ideas

One of the statements below expresses the main idea of the passage. One statement is too general, or too broad. The other explains only part of the passage; it is too narrow. Label the statements M for *main idea,* B for *too broad,* and N for *too narrow.*

_____ a. The family members shown in *Migrant Mother* have tattered clothing.

_____ b. Many photographs of the Great Depression reveal the pain that people suffered during that time.

_____ c. Photojournalist Dorothea Lange's photographs, such as her *Migrant Mother,* documented the suffering in the Great Depression.

Correct Answers, Part A _____

Correct Answers, Part B _____

Total Correct Answers _____

City Management: Responsibilities of a Mayor

A mayor is elected to help run a city. The mayor makes sure that a city functions properly—not an easy job. A mayor must keep track of all city activities. Mayors, however, do not work alone. They share the responsibilities of city government with city councils.

There are two types of mayors: "weak" and "strong." In cities that use a weak-mayor system, the city council holds most of the power. Under this system, the council members and some department heads are elected by the people. The council prepares the city budget, hires and fires city employees, and appoints heads of city departments. There can be many boards and committees. Each group is responsible for one city department. Although the mayor is elected, he or she has little power. The weak mayor may recommend appointments to city departments, yet these appointments must be approved by the council. In most cases, the mayor cannot veto, or override, a council decision.

In a strong-mayor system, the elected mayor is the city's chief executive. The mayor appoints all the department heads. He or she makes sure that the heads of these departments run them efficiently. The elected city council does not have the power to approve the mayor's appointments. The council cannot veto an appointment. However, the mayor does have the right to veto decisions made by the council.

Strong mayors oversee various city departments. These include fire, police, health, and transportation departments. Some mayors also oversee the city-planning department. This department plans the way in which the city will grow and develop. In a large city, such as New York, the mayor may also oversee departments of cultural affairs, prisons, parks, consumer affairs, immigration, and environment. New York's mayor is also responsible for naming judges to city courts and making sure that the laws are enforced.

A strong mayor prepares the city budget, so in this sense the mayor funds city services. Citizens know whom to blame if services fail. The mayor works with the council, however, to identify the city's needs and carry out city projects.

Strong mayors have considerable say, within legal limits, in how a city should be run. City laws are often written into a charter. A city's charter sets forth how the city and its departments are to be organized. It also spells out the duties of the mayor and other officials.

Reading Time _____

Recalling Facts

1. The job of mayor is filled through
   - ❑ a. election.
   - ❑ b. appointment.
   - ❑ c. departments.

2. Weak mayors do not always have
   - ❑ a. city councils.
   - ❑ b. employees.
   - ❑ c. a council veto.

3. A city budget contains instructions for
   - ❑ a. raising taxes.
   - ❑ b. funding city services.
   - ❑ c. hiring and firing city workers.

4. Most decisions in cities with weak mayors are made by
   - ❑ a. department heads.
   - ❑ b. a strong mayor.
   - ❑ c. the city council.

5. What a strong mayor can do is limited by
   - ❑ a. the taxation department.
   - ❑ b. the city charter.
   - ❑ c. the city council's veto.

Understanding Ideas

6. One can infer that a strong mayor oversees
   - ❑ a. maintenance of roads and highways.
   - ❑ b. the amount of money the city gets from the state.
   - ❑ c. the rulings made by judges.

7. One difference in responsibilities between a strong city mayor and a weak city mayor is that
   - ❑ a. weak mayors' cities do not have charters.
   - ❑ b. weak mayors are not elected.
   - ❑ c. strong mayors control the city budget.

8. If things go wrong in a city with a strong mayor system, one can predict that citizens
   - ❑ a. will not reelect the mayor.
   - ❑ b. will fire the heads of city departments.
   - ❑ c. will demand changes in the city charter.

9. The author of this passage would most likely agree that
   - ❑ a. a weak mayor of a small city has little to do.
   - ❑ b. a mayor has a demanding job.
   - ❑ c. states give cities too little money.

10. If a weak mayor's appointment of a department head is not approved, the reason is probably that
    - ❑ a. the department has been abolished.
    - ❑ b. the city council has vetoed the appointment.
    - ❑ c. without money, the department has been unable to function.

Fiorello LaGuardia was mayor of New York City from 1934 to 1945. Because of his first name, he was known as the "Little Flower." (The word *fiore* is Italian for "flower".) He was only 5 feet 2 inches tall, but his big heart and character made up for his height.

LaGuardia was born in 1882. At 17 he worked in Europe for the U.S. government. When he came home, he went to law school. He graduated in 1910. Elected to Congress in 1916, he soon left to be a pilot in World War I. He returned to Congress in 1923.

LaGuardia was elected mayor in 1934. He vowed to clean up city corruption. He began a huge reform program. LaGuardia's honesty restored people's faith in city government. He showed he was a great leader by attracting the best people into city government. Under his dynamic leadership, much was accomplished. This man of the people had schools, hospitals, bridges, and low-income housing built.

LaGuardia's personality endeared him to New Yorkers. He had his own weekly radio show. During one newspaper strike, LaGuardia read the comics over the air to his delighted audience. Sometimes he showed up to conduct the city orchestra. Because of such traits, Fiorello LaGuardia is regarded by many as New York City's greatest mayor.

1. Recognizing Words in Context

Find the word *dynamic* in the passage. One definition below is closest to the meaning of that word. One definition has the opposite or nearly the opposite meaning. The remaining definition has a completely different meaning. Label the definitions C for *closest*, O for *opposite or nearly opposite*, and D for *different*.

_____ a. energetic

_____ b. corrupt

_____ c. lazy

2. Distinguishing Fact from Opinion

Two of the statements below present *facts*, which can be proved. The other statement is an *opinion*, which expresses someone's thoughts or beliefs. Label the statements F for *fact* and O for *opinion*.

_____ a. LaGuardia was elected to Congress twice.

_____ b. LaGuardia fought corruption in New York City.

_____ c. New Yorkers loved LaGuardia.

3. Keeping Events in Order

Number the statements below 1, 2, and 3 to show the order in which the events took place.

_____ a. LaGuardia served as mayor of New York City.

_____ b. LaGuardia served the government in Europe.

_____ c. LaGuardia was elected to Congress.

4. Making Correct Inferences

Two of the statements below are correct *inferences,* or reasonable guesses. They are based on information in the passage. The other statement is an incorrect, or faulty, inference. Label the statements C for *correct* inference and F for *faulty* inference.

_____ a. LaGuardia was a popular politician.

_____ b. LaGuardia enjoyed music.

_____ c. LaGuardia missed being in Congress.

5. Understanding Main Ideas

One of the statements below expresses the main idea of the passage. One statement is too general, or too broad. The other explains only part of the passage; it is too narrow. Label the statements M for *main idea,* B for *too broad,* and N for *too narrow.*

_____ a. LaGuardia was mayor of New York City for more than 10 years.

_____ b. LaGuardia was an effective, respected, energetic New York mayor.

_____ c. Mayors of New York, such as Fiorello LaGuardia and Rudolph Guiliani, have had to work with citizens to solve challenging problems.

Correct Answers, Part A _____

Correct Answers, Part B _____

Total Correct Answers _____

The Plains Indians and the Buffalo

Many Native peoples live in the United States. Several groups of Plains Indians make their home in the Great Plains region. Three of these are the Sioux, the Cheyenne, and the Arapaho. The culture of the Plains Indian is known for the importance of the bison, or buffalo, once their single most vital resource. It was also part of the Native nations religions. They believed that the buffalo was sacred, and they respected the animal because it clothed and fed them. The buffalo was a symbol of inner strength. It reminded the people that all creatures depend on one another for survival.

The Plains Indians hunted many animals, but the buffalo was by far the most important to them, so they never killed more than they needed. They would track the animals' movements. They performed special songs and dances when they saw a herd. The dancers wore masks of an entire buffalo head during the dancing. After these ceremonies, the warriors began the hunt. The most common way of hunting the buffalo was on horseback. The men used bows and arrows. While the men were hunting, the women set up the camp. Once the hunters killed a buffalo, the women and children helped to carry it back to camp.

The people did not waste any part of the buffalo. They used the meat for food. It could be dried and kept for a long time. They used the skin for clothing and for making tepees and blankets. Buffalo skin could also be stretched and made into boats. They made spoons and cups with the horns and tools from buffalo bones. The stomach and intestines were cleaned and used to carry water in. Buffalo hooves were boiled and made into glue. Sinew, which is in the muscles of the backbone, served as thread for sewing. Sinew could also be used to make webbing in snowshoes. Buffalo teeth became ornaments on jewelry. Women made soap, candles, and hair grease from the fat. The buffalo beard decorated clothes. The tail was used as a fly swatter or a whip.

The buffalo skull played an important role in religious ceremonies. It served as an altar at which people presented offerings. The eyes and nose were stuffed with grass to symbolize vegetation. If there was enough vegetation, the buffalo that they found would be healthy—and healthy buffalo meant that the people would have enough to eat.

Reading Time _____

Recalling Facts

1. One of the Plains Indians tribes is the
   - ❏ a. Sioux.
   - ❏ b. Cherokee.
   - ❏ c. Navajo.

2. The buffalo was a symbol of the spiritual value of
   - ❏ a. inner strength.
   - ❏ b. peace.
   - ❏ c. justice.

3. Buffalo bones were used to make _____ from.
   - ❏ a. spoons
   - ❏ b. arrow heads
   - ❏ c. tools

4. The part of the buffalo used in religious ceremonies was the
   - ❏ a. hoof.
   - ❏ b. skull.
   - ❏ c. tail.

5. Sinew comes from buffalo
   - ❏ a. bones.
   - ❏ b. muscles.
   - ❏ c. teeth.

Understanding Ideas

6. One can conclude from the passage that the role of the buffalo in the Plains Indians' religions stemmed from
   - ❏ a. its importance for survival.
   - ❏ b. the huge size of the animal.
   - ❏ c. the shape of its skull.

7. If the Plains Indians could not find buffalo to hunt, it is likely that
   - ❏ a. they changed their religion.
   - ❏ b. there was little change in their condition.
   - ❏ c. they suffered.

8. Which of the following statements is most likely true?
   - ❏ a. Because buffalo are again plentiful in the United States, they are still widely used by people for food and clothing.
   - ❏ b. The buffalo is more important to the Plains Indians today than it was in the nineteenth century.
   - ❏ c. When the buffalo herds began to vanish, the Plains Indians had to change their way of life.

9. One can conclude from the passage that the Plains Indians
   - ❏ a. were very resourceful.
   - ❏ b. were very wasteful.
   - ❏ c. cared little about their environment.

10. Which statement most closely supports the philosophy of the Plains Indians?
    - ❏ a. Only the strongest creatures will survive.
    - ❏ b. Each person must look after him or herself.
    - ❏ c. If the balance of nature is upset, all creatures will suffer.

A Native American celebration is called a powwow. A powwow can be any type of celebration. It can be a religious ceremony or a family reunion. In modern times, powwows are annual summer gatherings that center on dancing. This is the Native people's way of talking with the Great Spirit.

One important powwow for Native Americans of the Plains is the Sun Dance. The Sun Dance lasts for four days. It is held at the time of the summer solstice. The dance shows the link between life and death. The Plains Indians believe that all creatures are connected to one another. This belief is essential to their religion because they believe that all creatures rely on one another for survival. No one creature is more important than any other one.

The Sun Dance also provides a way for the Plains Indians to honor the sacredness of the buffalo. The Indians have always held the buffalo sacred. In the past, however, they had to kill it for food. This was a conflict of principles. The dancers of the Sun Dance sacrificed through fasting and thirsting. They also inflicted pain on themselves. These torments were intended to honor the spirit of the buffalo. In 1904 the U.S. government outlawed the Sun Dance. Today some native groups have brought back variations of this ceremony.

1. **Recognizing Words in Context**

   Find the word *conflict* in the passage. One definition below is closest to the meaning of that word. One definition has the opposite or nearly the opposite meaning. The remaining definition has a completely different meaning. Label the definitions C for *closest*, O for *opposite or nearly opposite,* and D for *different.*

   _____ a. agreement

   _____ b. clash

   _____ c. invitation

2. **Distinguishing Fact from Opinion**

   Two of the statements below present *facts,* which can be proved. The other statement is an *opinion,* which expresses someone's thoughts or beliefs. Label the statements F for *fact* and O for *opinion.*

   _____ a. The buffalo was very important to the Plains Indians.

   _____ b. Everyone considers the celebrations of the Plains Indians interesting.

   _____ c. A celebration is also called a powwow.

3. **Keeping Events in Order**

Number the statements below 1, 2, and 3 to show the order in which the events took place.

_____ a. The United States government outlawed the Sun Dance.

_____ b. The Plains Indians held the traditional Sun Dance.

_____ c. The Plains Indians revived variations of the Sun Dance.

4. **Making Correct Inferences**

Two of the statements below are correct *inferences,* or reasonable guesses. They are based on information in the passage. The other statement is an incorrect, or faulty, inference. Label the statements C for *correct* inference and F for *faulty* inference.

_____ a. The summer solstice has symbolic meaning for the Plains Indians.

_____ b. Powwows are religious celebrations, not social celebrations.

_____ c. Dancing is an important part of Native American cultures.

5. **Understanding Main Ideas**

One of the statements below expresses the main idea of the passage. One statement is too general, or too broad. The other explains only part of the passage; it is too narrow. Label the statements M for *main idea,* B for *too broad,* and N for *too narrow.*

_____ a. Dancers in the Sun Dance fasted to honor the spirit of the buffalo.

_____ b. A powwow is a Native American celebration.

_____ c. The Sun Dance powwow is an important part of life for the Plains Indians.

Correct Answers, Part A _____

Correct Answers, Part B _____

Total Correct Answers _____

The Middle Ages in Europe was a difficult period. Everyday life was harsh, and thieves and animals presented dangers. For protection, a community grew up in a central place called a manor.

The manor consisted of a castle, a church, the village, and nearby farmland. Every manor had a lord, who was in charge. Most people living in the manor were peasants. The manor system allowed the peasants to have land to farm, but the lord heavily taxed the peasants. The peasants had to give him most of their crops. In exchange the lord protected the peasants from thieves and soldiers passing through. This protection was valuable in those dangerous times. Such a system of society was called feudalism. The lord was at the top of the system, and the peasants, or serfs, were at the bottom.

A peasant man could be expected to spend up to 18 hours each day in the fields. A peasant woman spent her day around the house. She tended the garden and cared for the family livestock. She also spun thread for cloth, which was used to make clothing. She made candles from tallow and cooked all of the meals. Children were also expected to work. Once a boy reached 10 years of age, he went to the fields. Girls stayed with their mothers and learned to do domestic chores. Peasants ate whatever they could grow, so it was very important that they work hard. Their main crops were corn, beets, and wheat. Sometimes the weather was poor, and crops were lost. Many people starved to death.

Most peasant homes were cold and dark, with thatched roofs and dirt floors. The walls were made of mud-plastered branches or of stone and wood. If there were windows, they were very small, because only the wealthy could afford panes of glass. In the winter, livestock were moved inside for warmth. There usually were only two rooms. A kitchen hearth, which served for both cooking and heating, was in the main room. Peasants commonly ate breads and vegetables from their gardens. They slept on stacks of straw. In the fall, animals were slaughtered, and the meat was used all year round.

There were many celebrations, however. People celebrated births and marriages, and religious holidays were a chance for a feast. Sometimes the lord of the manor provided for the feast. At those times there was dancing and food for all.

Reading Time _____

Recalling Facts

1. Most people in the Middle Ages were
   - ❑ a. manor lords.
   - ❑ b. thieves.
   - ❑ c. peasants.

2. A peasant man or boy spent most of his time
   - ❑ a. in the office.
   - ❑ b. in the fields.
   - ❑ c. hunting for food.

3. The manor was often made up of the castle, the church, the village, and the
   - ❑ a. farmland.
   - ❑ b. railroad station.
   - ❑ c. harbor.

4. The type of social system that evolved in the Middle Ages was called
   - ❑ a. an educational system.
   - ❑ b. feudalism.
   - ❑ c. a proprietary system.

5. The floors in a peasant home were made of
   - ❑ a. dirt.
   - ❑ b. wood.
   - ❑ c. stone.

Understanding Ideas

6. One can conclude from the passage that
   - ❑ a. peasants benefited most from feudalism.
   - ❑ b. lords benefited most from feudalism.
   - ❑ c. peasants and lords received equal benefit from feudalism.

7. It is most likely that a peasant farmer
   - ❑ a. would one day be a manor lord.
   - ❑ b. would one day be able to start his own farm.
   - ❑ c. would always remain a peasant farmer.

8. One born in the Middle Ages would most likely have been a
   - ❑ a. peasant.
   - ❑ b. manor lord.
   - ❑ c. priest.

9. One can conclude from the passage that life for most people in the Middle Ages
   - ❑ a. was very relaxing.
   - ❑ b. provided time for the pursuit of education.
   - ❑ c. involved a great deal of physical labor.

10. Which of the following sentences best tells what the passage is about?
    - ❑ a. People in the Middle Ages had celebrations for births and marriages.
    - ❑ b. Life in the Middle Ages involved many hardships for the average person.
    - ❑ c. A lord in the Middle Ages was in charge of a manor.

Medieval Clothing

In the Middle Ages, clothing styles depended on a person's role in society. People were not permitted to wear whatever they liked; each class wore its own kind of clothes.

Kings and queens wore bright, vibrant colors. Queens often wore fancy headpieces. Some of the fabrics used were silk and damask. Men of the nobility wore hose and jackets; a longer jacket was a sign of wealth. Women of this class wore flowing gowns. Like the queen, they often wore fancy headpieces. The clothes of the wealthy were made by tailors, and only those of high rank wore jewelry. The ring brooch was the most common type of jewelry. In the fourteenth century, diamonds became very popular; but by the mid-fourteenth century, laws were created that determined who could wear what kind of jewelry.

Peasants wore any clothing that they could find or make. Their clothes were rough and shapeless, and the colors were mainly gray and brown. Peasants were most interested in keeping warm and dry. Their clothes were usually made of wool, which they spun themselves, and their undergarments were made of linen.

Members of holy orders, such as priests, monks, and nuns, wore long woolen hoods and habits, tied with a rope belt with wooden beads. A person could tell what order someone belonged to by the color of the habit.

1. Recognizing Words in Context

Find the word *vibrant* in the passage. One definition below is closest to the meaning of that word. One definition has the opposite or nearly the opposite meaning. The remaining definition has a completely different meaning. Label the definitions C for *closest*, O for *opposite or nearly opposite,* and D for *different.*

_____ a. dry

_____ b. lively

_____ c. dull

2. Distinguishing Fact from Opinion

Two of the statements below present *facts*, which can be proved. The other statement is an *opinion*, which expresses someone's thoughts or beliefs. Label the statements F for *fact* and O for *opinion.*

_____ a. The peasants' clothing in the Middle Ages was unattractive.

_____ b. In the Middle Ages, kings and queens wore silk clothing.

_____ c. In the Middle Ages, a longer jacket identified a person of high rank.

3. **Keeping Events in Order**

Number the statements below 1, 2, and 3 to show the order in which the events took place.

_____ a. Only those of high rank could wear diamonds.

_____ b. Laws determined the type of jewelry that could be worn.

_____ c. Diamonds became very popular.

4. **Making Correct Inferences**

Two of the statements below are correct *inferences,* or reasonable guesses. They are based on information in the passage. The other statement is an incorrect, or faulty, inference. Label the statements C for *correct* inference and F for *faulty* inference.

_____ a. Tailors made clothing for all classes of people.

_____ b. Peasants did not have many kinds of clothing.

_____ c. The clothing of the wealthy was more colorful than that of the peasants.

5. **Understanding Main Ideas**

One of the statements below expresses the main idea of the passage. One statement is too general, or too broad. The other explains only part of the passage; it is too narrow. Label the statements M for *main idea,* B for *too broad,* and N for *too narrow.*

_____ a. Clothing in the Middle Ages was determined by social status.

_____ b. Queens wore fancy headpieces.

_____ c. Clothing styles have changed in every century, including the Middle Ages.

Correct Answers, Part A _____

Correct Answers, Part B _____

Total Correct Answers _____

The countries that make up the European Union (EU) have not always been friends. In the past, they often were at war. At the end of the most recent war, in 1945, some people decided that it was time for a change. It would be better, they thought, to work together than to compete. The EU began as a federation in 1950. At the time, it had 6 members. Today its membership stands at 15.

Building the union was no easy task. Each nation had to prove to its citizens that such a union was a good idea. Finally, in 1993, most of the countries signed a formal treaty. This treaty created the EU. Since then, they have worked together as a union. They have improved trade and increased wealth. They also cooperate on such matters as the law and foreign relations. In 1998 EU members agreed to create a single form of money that is legal tender for them all.

The money used by most countries of the EU is called the euro. It came into use on the first day of 2002. The sign for the euro ( ) resembles a capital E. One euro is 100 euro cents. There are eight coins and seven banknotes. The coins range from 1 cent up to 2 euros. The banknotes are worth from 5 to 500 euros.

One could say that the euro coin is an emblem of the union of different cultures. On one side of the coin is a map of Europe. There are also stars that stand for the member countries. Each nation chooses a special design for the other side. Every Netherlands coin has a picture of its queen on it, for example. Italy pictures some of its famous works of art. All of the banknotes are alike. Any coin can be used in any country that has switched to the new euro.

Twelve of the nations in the EU now use the euro. Three countries—Denmark, Sweden, and the United Kingdom—still use their own money. These three countries may, however, start using the euro at a later time.

The new system is useful for companies that do business in more than one country in the EU. It is also helpful for people who travel. A person who plans to visit Paris, Athens, and Madrid, for instance, no longer has to learn about French francs, Greek drachmas, and Spanish pesetas.

Reading Time _____

Recalling Facts

1. The Euro is the money
   - ❑ a. replaced by the franc in France and the peseta in Spain.
   - ❑ b. used by most countries of the European Union.
   - ❑ c. given travelers who are leaving Europe.

2. Each euro coin
   - ❑ a. has a design on one side that is chosen by a member nation.
   - ❑ b. is worth a euro cent.
   - ❑ c. can be used in only one country.

3. The new euro system is helpful for
   - ❑ a. countries that do business outside Europe.
   - ❑ b. people who do not travel.
   - ❑ c. companies that do business in more than one European country.

4. Among the countries that use the euro are
   - ❑ a. the United Kingdom and Spain.
   - ❑ b. Denmark and Sweden.
   - ❑ c. Greece, Italy, and the Netherlands.

5. One of the problems people faced in creating the European Union was that
   - ❑ a. nobody was interested in the project.
   - ❑ b. most countries already used the euro.
   - ❑ c. countries that had been enemies had to work together.

Understanding Ideas

6. One can conclude from the passage that money that is legal tender
   - ❑ a. has to be changed into real money before being used.
   - ❑ b. is the official money of a country.
   - ❑ c. is almost worthless.

7. It is likely that it took so long to agree on a single currency because
   - ❑ a. there was not much trade between the countries of the EU.
   - ❑ b. most nations refused to cooperate with the EU.
   - ❑ c. each country considered its money a form of national identity.

8. Which of the following opinions is probably shared by EU members?
   - ❑ a. Making financial transactions easier will not affect trade.
   - ❑ b. Cutthroat competition among members will result in a stronger EU.
   - ❑ c. Shared prosperity is better than mutual devastation.

9. One can conclude that EU nations that saw each other as enemies could not share a common currency until
   - ❑ a. they built trust over time.
   - ❑ b. they decided on a common form of government.
   - ❑ c. they agreed to speak one language.

10. The primary motivation for creating the European Union was probably
   - ❑ a. philosophical.
   - ❑ b. cultural.
   - ❑ c. economic.

20 B   Travel and Money

Planning a trip through Europe? It is important to think about money. It can be difficult to estimate how much one is spending. A wallet that is lost or stolen also can create problems. So what issues should one think about in advance?

Experienced travelers start by learning about the money they will be using in a foreign country. Most of Europe now uses the euro. Like the dollar, one euro equals 100 cents. However, one dollar and one euro are not the same thing. The difference in value between the dollar and the euro is called the exchange rate. This rate changes every day. Check at a bank or on the Internet to find out the exchange rate.

What is the safest way to carry money? Everyone agrees that it is imprudent to carry large amounts of cash. Many travelers prefer to carry travelers' checks. Travelers' checks can be used in many places around the world instead of cash. Travelers can also exchange them for the local money. If they are lost or stolen, it is possible to get them replaced. Some people would rather get cash from their bank accounts by using an automated teller machine. This device allows people to get only as much cash as they need. They have to be careful, however, not to lose their bankcards.

1. **Recognizing Words in Context**

   Find the word *imprudent* in the passage. One definition below is closest to the meaning of that word. One definition has the opposite or nearly the opposite meaning. The remaining definition has a completely different meaning. Label the definitions C for *closest*, O for *opposite or nearly opposite*, and D for *different*.

   _____ a. sensible

   _____ b. unwise

   _____ c. imperfect

2. **Distinguishing Fact from Opinion**

   Two of the statements below present *facts*, which can be proved. The other statement is an *opinion*, which expresses someone's thoughts or beliefs. Label the statements F for *fact* and O for *opinion*.

   _____ a. Travelers' checks can be used in many places instead of cash.

   _____ b. It is unwise to carry large amounts of cash.

   _____ c. Most of Europe uses the euro.

3. Keeping Events in Order

Number the instructions below 1, 2, and 3 to show the order in which they should be followed.

_____ a. Check the Internet to find out the exchange rate.

_____ b. Use travelers' checks to pay for purchases.

_____ c. Decide on your travel destination.

4. Making Correct Inferences

Two of the statements below are correct *inferences,* or reasonable guesses. They are based on information in the passage. The other statement is an incorrect, or faulty, inference. Label the statements C for *correct* inference and F for *faulty* inference.

_____ a. Knowing the exchange rate ensures knowing how much something costs in another country.

_____ b. The bankcard one uses in the United States can probably be used at banks in Europe.

_____ c. Traveling in Europe is dangerous.

5. Understanding Main Ideas

One of the statements below expresses the main idea of the passage. One statement is too general, or too broad. The other explains only part of the passage; it is too narrow. Label the statements M for *main idea,* B for *too broad,* and N for *too narrow.*

_____ a. If travelers' checks are lost or stolen, they can be replaced.

_____ b. Learning about the exchange rate and the safest way to carry money is important when planning a trip to a foreign country.

_____ c. Careful preparation is important to ensure a successful trip to a foreign country.

Correct Answers, Part A _____

Correct Answers, Part B _____

Total Correct Answers _____

21   A   Keeping Workers Safe on the Job

Workplaces in the United States were once very dangerous because they were governed by no formal safety laws. Officials thought that private businesses should set their own rules. Many business owners were more concerned with profits, however, than with safety. This attitude sometimes led to unsafe working conditions.

In 1911 the Triangle Shirtwaist Fire took place in New York City. This tragedy, and others like it, angered people. The New York legislature began to look into working conditions in buildings. The Division of Fire Prevention was created to rid buildings of fire hazards. It developed new fire codes. For instance, the new fire code required that all doors open outward. They also had to remain unlocked during business hours. Businesses having more than 25 workers had to install sprinkler systems. Fire escapes had to be able to carry the weight of workers. These and other codes helped to ensure a safe workplace for all.

There are other safety issues besides fire danger. In 1970 Congress passed the Occupational Safety and Health Act, which states that all people have the right to a safe and healthful workplace. The Occupational Safety and Health Administration (OSHA) was formed. OSHA has had a great impact on the workplace. It sets and enforces workplace safety laws. It provides workers with safety and health facts and information and also helps employers to comply with safety codes. OSHA can help workers who think that their workplace is unsafe. Any worker may file a complaint with OSHA.

OSHA provides safety rules. This agency also helps to keep workers safe in other ways. One way is by requiring them to wear safety gear such as goggles or gloves. Another is by limiting the contact a worker has with harmful chemicals.

OSHA helps to save lives and prevent harm in the workplace. Since 1970 workplace deaths have declined 50 percent. In 1988 job-related injury and illness rates were the lowest on record. However, for 100 million workers and 6 million work sites in the United States, there are only about 2,500 OSHA inspectors. Workers must take an active role in their own safety. They should comply with posted safety rules, and they should report any breach of rules right away. If possible, employees and employers should work together to resolve safety issues. Sometimes an employer refuses to make needed changes. OSHA can then be called in to enforce federal standards.

Reading Time _____

Recalling Facts

1. Working conditions before the establishment of OSHA were
   - ❏ a. not so safe as they are today.
   - ❏ b. very safe.
   - ❏ c. a high priority to business owners.

2. The Occupational Safety and Health Act was passed in
   - ❏ a. 1911.
   - ❏ b. 1988.
   - ❏ c. 1970.

3. Keeping all doors unlocked during business hours is an example of
   - ❏ a. air-quality control.
   - ❏ b. a fire-safety code.
   - ❏ c. being overly cautious.

4. The Occupational Safety and Health Act was passed by
   - ❏ a. the president of the United States.
   - ❏ b. the governor of New York.
   - ❏ c. Congress.

5. An example of required safety equipment is
   - ❏ a. woolen socks.
   - ❏ b. goggles.
   - ❏ c. a wristwatch.

Understanding Ideas

6. One can conclude from the passage that workplace safety
   - ❏ a. will not be a concern in the future.
   - ❏ b. will continue to improve.
   - ❏ c. will begin to decline.

7. From the passage, one can conclude that
   - ❏ a. unsafe conditions were responsible for the Triangle Shirtwaist Fire tragedy.
   - ❏ b. the Triangle Shirtwaist Fire was the work of an arsonist.
   - ❏ c. the Triangle Shirtwaist Fire was an unusual incident.

8. Compared with workplaces in the nineteenth century, workplaces today are
   - ❏ a. safer.
   - ❏ b. less safe.
   - ❏ c. about as safe as they were then.

9. It is likely that Congress passed federal laws to mandate workplace safety
   - ❏ a. at the insistence of business owners.
   - ❏ b. before a factory disaster occurred.
   - ❏ c. because of incidents such as the Triangle Shirtwaist Fire.

10. In order to ensure workplace safety, one can conclude that
    - ❏ a. fewer regulations are needed by OSHA.
    - ❏ b. everyone ultimately must take responsibility for his or her own safety.
    - ❏ c. a representative from OSHA should be employed by every company.

In early 1911, the Triangle Shirtwaist Company was in business in New York City. It employed almost 500 people. Many of these were young women between 19 and 23 years old. Many were immigrants. They had come from other countries hoping for a better life.

Work at the factory was hard. Workers were paid little for their time. They worked long hours. On March 25, shortly after 4:30 P.M., fire broke out in the factory. At the time, 275 women were in the building, and 146 died.

Some or all of these deaths probably could have been avoided. The building had no safety procedures. Doors opened inward instead of outward. The building had no sprinkler systems. Many of the doors were locked. This trapped the victims in the fire because they were unable to open the doors to escape. There were only 27 buckets of water to douse the fire. Fire hoses and ladders did not reach beyond the seventh floor. The fire escapes could not support the weight of the workers trying to leave. The fire escapes collapsed, trapping the workers inside the burning building.

The Triangle Shirtwaist Fire was the worst fire in the history of New York up to that time. As a result of this fire, many important safety regulations were put into place in the United States.

1. **Recognizing Words in Context**

   Find the word *douse* in the passage. One definition below is closest to the meaning of that word. One definition has the opposite or nearly the opposite meaning. The remaining definition has a completely different meaning. Label the definitions C for *closest,* O for *opposite or nearly opposite,* and D for *different.*

   _____ a. drench

   _____ b. throw off

   _____ c. make do

2. **Distinguishing Fact from Opinion**

   Two of the statements below present *facts,* which can be proved. The other statement is an *opinion,* which expresses someone's thoughts or beliefs. Label the statements F for *fact* and O for *opinion.*

   _____ a. The Triangle Shirtwaist Company had no safety procedures.

   _____ b. The Triangle Shirtwaist Company factory did not provide means of escape.

   _____ c. The Triangle Shirtwaist Company was concerned only with making a profit.

3. Keeping Events in Order

Number the statements below 1, 2, and 3 to show the order in which the events took place.

_____ a. One hundred forty-six workers died.

_____ b. Employees were working at the Triangle Shirtwaist Company.

_____ c. Fire broke out in the building.

4. Making Correct Inferences

Two of the statements below are correct *inferences,* or reasonable guesses. They are based on information in the passage. The other statement is an incorrect, or faulty, inference. Label the statements C for *correct* inference and F for *faulty* inference.

_____ a. Having safety procedures in place can help prevent worker deaths.

_____ b. All workplace deaths can be prevented.

_____ c. Workplaces can be dangerous.

5. Understanding Main Ideas

One of the statements below expresses the main idea of the passage. One statement is too general, or too broad. The other explains only part of the passage; it is too narrow. Label the statements M for *main idea*, B for *too broad,* and N for *too narrow.*

_____ a. The Triangle Shirtwaist fire was a devastating event that had long-term effects on building-safety regulations.

_____ b. Most employees at the Triangle Shirtwaist Company were women.

_____ c. A factory can be an unsafe place to work.

Correct Answers, Part A _____

Correct Answers, Part B _____

Total Correct Answers _____

Farming and Towns in the Ancient Middle East

Farming began thousands of years ago in the Middle East, which is part of Asia. The Middle East extends from the Fertile Crescent in the east to the Mediterranean Sea in the west. The Fertile Crescent is the rich arc of land bordered by the Tigris (tī´gris) and Euphrates (yoo frā´ tēz) rivers. The Middle East is not only the first place where human beings grew crops. It is also the site of some of the world's first great cities and cultures. For some peoples, farming was just one of many ways to produce food. They were neither just hunters nor just farmers. They were a bit of both. For others farming became an important part of the culture.

How did farming come about? No one knows for sure. Ancient peoples were as much a part of the natural world as the beasts in the forests and the birds in the skies. They were keen observers of life around them. It is likely that they noticed that plants grew from seeds fallen on the ground. The first step toward farming was to gather the plants where they grew in the wild. The next step was to collect seeds and plant them nearer home.

The first crops were grains such as barley and wheat. These grains could be dried and stored for a long time, giving the ancient farmer something to eat when hunting was poor.

When fields produced food, people settled down and built homes. A secure food supply meant that they lived longer and had more children. Larger numbers of people turned small villages into towns and cities. In other words, in some places the practice of farming brought about the start of towns. In other areas, towns were formed before farming became important. In these places, people may have turned to farming because hunting and gathering no longer supplied enough food.

By the beginning of the Neolithic Age, about 10,000 years ago, both farms and populations began to flourish. More food supported increasing numbers of people. People could then produce even more food. During this time, also called the New Stone Age, people began to domesticate animals. Rather than rely on hunting, people now raised animals for food. Some scholars call the changes connected to farming the Neolithic Revolution. Within about 2,000 years, farmers in the Middle East were growing different kinds of grain, as well as vegetables such as lentils and peas.

Reading Time _____

Recalling Facts

1. It is believed that farming began thousands of years ago
   - ❑ a. in the Middle East.
   - ❑ b. alongside the Rhine River.
   - ❑ c. in Europe.

2. The first crops planted by people were
   - ❑ a. vegetables such as lentils and peas.
   - ❑ b. grains such as barley and wheat.
   - ❑ c. fruit trees.

3. A secure food supply
   - ❑ a. caused people to move from place to place.
   - ❑ b. was provided by hunting.
   - ❑ c. allowed people to live longer and have more children.

4. Another name for the Neolithic period is the
   - ❑ a. New Stone Age.
   - ❑ b. Fertile Crescent.
   - ❑ c. Middle Ages.

5. The Fertile Crescent is
   - ❑ a. located in Europe.
   - ❑ b. the land bordered by the Tigris and Euphrates rivers.
   - ❑ c. alongside the Mediterranean Sea.

Understanding Ideas

6. One can conclude that farming
   - ❑ a. replaced hunting in the Neolithic Period.
   - ❑ b. is a modern discovery in the Middle East.
   - ❑ c. seems connected to the growth of towns in the Middle East.

7. From the passage, one can infer that
   - ❑ a. advances in food production had little impact on people.
   - ❑ b. advances in food production led to changes in living.
   - ❑ c. farming did not result in more food in the Neolithic Period.

8. Farming became an important part of human culture
   - ❑ a. about the time that people learned to hunt.
   - ❑ b. only after hunting and gathering no longer supplied enough food.
   - ❑ c. at different times for different groups.

9. When one says that farms and populations began to "flourish," it means that
   - ❑ a. farms and people increased.
   - ❑ b. life became a great struggle.
   - ❑ c. most people moved out of towns and into cities.

10. The expression "Neolithic Revolution" describes the
    - ❑ a. war that broke out between Neolithic groups.
    - ❑ b. increase in farming and rapid growth of towns that took place during that time.
    - ❑ c. discovery that metal tools were better for hunting and farming.

Çatal Hüyük

Çatal Hüyük (kət äl´ hə yoŏk´) was once a grand city in the Middle East. Built in central Turkey about 8,000 years ago, it was a large city for its time. Most of the people who lived there were farmers. They grew crops and raised sheep and cattle. It was also a center for trade in obsidian (əb si´ dē ən), black glass that was collected from nearby volcanoes.

Çatal Hüyük was built without any streets. Mud-brick buildings were connected around a central courtyard. To enter a building, one had to climb through a hole in the roof and down a ladder. The inside walls and ceilings were painted, often in red, with patterns and pictures of animals. Each house had a hearth for cooking and heat. Platforms made from mud bricks were used as beds or work areas. Religion was very important. One out of every four buildings seems to have been used for worship. These spaces were often bigger than the houses. The wall paintings were larger and more ornate than in the living areas. The town's outside walls were thick and solid to protect it from attack.

Çatal Hüyük was a busy city for about 1,000 years. Then suddenly it was abandoned. It was almost forgotten until a British archaeologist, James Mellaart, uncovered it in 1961.

1. **Recognizing Words in Context**

   Find the word *ornate* in the passage. One definition below is closest to the meaning of that word. One definition has the opposite or nearly the opposite meaning. The remaining definition has a completely different meaning. Label the definitions C for *closest*, O for *opposite or nearly opposite*, and D for *different*.

   _____ a. cautious

   _____ b. plain

   _____ c. decorative

2. **Distinguishing Fact from Opinion**

   Two of the statements below present *facts*, which can be proved. The other statement is an *opinion*, which expresses someone's thoughts or beliefs. Label the statements F for *fact* and O for *opinion*.

   _____ a. Çatal Hüyük was a city in the Middle East.

   _____ b. Çatal Hüyük was built without any streets.

   _____ c. Rooms used for worship were more beautiful than other spaces.

3. Keeping Events in Order

Number the statements below 1, 2, and 3 to show the order in which the events took place.

_____ a. Çatal Hüyük was abandoned.

_____ b. People living in Çatal Hüyük farmed and raised cattle.

_____ c. The archaeologist James Mellaart found Çatal Hüyük.

4. Making Correct Inferences

Two of the statements below are correct *inferences,* or reasonable guesses. They are based on information in the passage. The other statement is an incorrect, or faulty, inference. Label the statements C for *correct* inference and F for *faulty* inference.

_____ a. Çatal Hüyük was the only town built without streets.

_____ b. Çatal Hüyük was a safe and comfortable place in which to live.

_____ c. The people of Çatal Hüyük had enemies.

5. Understanding Main Ideas

One of the statements below expresses the main idea of the passage. One statement is too general, or too broad. The other explains only part of the passage; it is too narrow. Label the statements M for *main idea*, B for *too broad*, and N for *too narrow*.

_____ a. Historians study ancient cities such as Çatal Hüyük.

_____ b. Çatal Hüyük was an ancient center of trade in the Middle East for about a thousand years.

_____ c. People in Çatal Hüyük decorated the inside walls of buildings with paintings.

Correct Answers, Part A _____

Correct Answers, Part B _____

Total Correct Answers _____

Many sports that people play today were invented or became popular in Europe during the Renaissance of the fifteenth and sixteenth centuries. Some of the best known are golf, tennis, badminton, and bowls.

Golf was born in Scotland. It is believed that the ancient Scots played a game of hitting pebbles into rabbit holes with sticks. By the 1400s, this pastime had become known as golf. The aim of golf is to hit a ball into a hole in the distance. It is played on a huge, open area that contains obstacles such as sand traps, woods, and ponds. The player who gets the ball into the distant hole in the fewest strokes wins. Before the 1400s, Scots played golf anywhere and everywhere. Citizens who were in the way of a flying golf ball were injured. A law was passed requiring golfers to play in areas set aside as golf courses.

Tennis also gained popularity during the Renaissance. Tennis opponents stand on opposite sides of a net. The net is strung across the middle of a court. On the floor of the court are lines indicating the boundaries of play. To play, one player hits the ball with a racket. The ball must go over the net to the opponent's side. The other player must hit the ball back over the net. If one player hits a ball out of bounds, or if a ball bounces more than once before a player hits it, the opponent gains the point. The earliest form of tennis was played without rackets. Players hit the ball with their hands.

Badminton, which also arose during the Renaissance, is related to tennis. This game is played by hitting a shuttlecock, or birdie, over a net with a racket. The shuttlecock is lightweight. Historians believe that it developed from the Renaissance habit of storing bird feathers (used as writing quills) by sticking them into a cork.

Perhaps the most common Renaissance game was bowls, which could be played anywhere outdoors. A circular boundary was drawn on the ground. Then one player threw a small target ball, called a jack, into the circle. Each player had four larger balls, called bowls. One by one, the bowls were tossed into the circle. The player whose bowl came closest to the jack won the game. Bowls is still popular today, especially in Italy where it is called *bocce*.

Reading Time _____

Recalling Facts

1. Golf was first played
   - ❑ a. in ancient Rome.
   - ❑ b. in Scotland.
   - ❑ c. in the woods.

2. Several hits, or strokes, are needed to get a golf ball into the hole because
   - ❑ a. the ball is very small.
   - ❑ b. golf sticks are very thin and weak.
   - ❑ c. the hole is far away.

3. In the earliest form of tennis, balls were
   - ❑ a. hit with the hand.
   - ❑ b. made of horse hide.
   - ❑ c. always hit out of bounds.

4. The badminton shuttlecock developed from
   - ❑ a. the lightweight tennis ball.
   - ❑ b. the practice of boiling goose feathers.
   - ❑ c. the practice of storing writing quills in corks.

5. In bowls a player wins if his or her bowl
   - ❑ a. gets closest to the jack.
   - ❑ b. knocks the jack out of the circle.
   - ❑ c. becomes the target jack.

Understanding Ideas

6. Badminton is like tennis in that in both games
   - ❑ a. players hit shuttlecocks.
   - ❑ b. players use a racket to hit an object over a net.
   - ❑ c. the object hit by a player is not allowed to touch the ground.

7. From the description of badminton in the passage, one can assume that
   - ❑ a. most badminton players also played tennis.
   - ❑ b. the shuttlecock came to be used in a game by chance.
   - ❑ c. all badminton players also liked to bowl.

8. From the information about golf in the passage, one can conclude that
   - ❑ a. an obstacle on the course should be avoided.
   - ❑ b. golf was not played in Scotland before the 1400s.
   - ❑ c. pebbles replaced horsehide golf balls during the 1400s.

9. From information in the passage, one can conclude that _____ during the Renaissance.
   - ❑ a. people had no time to play games
   - ❑ b. competition was discouraged
   - ❑ c. sports were a popular pastime

10. Bowls is still the most popular sport among ordinary people in Europe, most likely because
    - ❑ a. it was invented in Italy.
    - ❑ b. it is simple and can be played anywhere.
    - ❑ c. players do not have to use a racket.

During the Renaissance, children played many simple games. One was called how-many-miles-to-London. In this game, a blindfolded child was "it." Players asked how many and what kind of steps they could take "to reach London." "It" told them what steps to take. Then "it" took the same steps and tried to touch another player. If touched, the player became "it."

Children also played hopscotch. Numbered boxes were drawn on the ground. Each player had a pebble. A child tossed the pebble into box 1. If it landed in the box, the child hopped from box to box in numerical order. A player who put two feet in one box, stepped on a line, or missed a box was out. If the player hopped through all of the boxes consecutively, he or she tossed the pebble into box 2 and hopped through the boxes again. The first player to toss the pebble into every numbered box and hop through them in sequence won.

Another popular game was row. It involved tossing small pebbles into holes. If a player's pebbles landed in holes that formed a straight line, he or she won. Tic-tac-toe is today's version of this game. Ninepins, in which children used a ball to knock down pins or bottles, has become today's bowling.

1. Recognizing Words in Context

Find the word *consecutively* in the passage. One definition below is closest to the meaning of that word. One definition has the opposite or nearly the opposite meaning. The remaining definition has a completely different meaning. Label the definitions C for *closest*, O for *opposite or nearly opposite*, and D for *different*.

_____ a. randomly

_____ b. sequentially

_____ c. boundlessly

2. Distinguishing Fact from Opinion

Two of the statements below present *facts*, which can be proved. The other statement is an *opinion*, which expresses someone's thoughts or beliefs. Label the statements F for *fact* and O for *opinion*.

_____ a. Hopscotch is the favorite game of most children.

_____ b. Bowling came from ninepins.

_____ c. A hopscotch player who stepped on a line was out.

3. Keeping Events in Order

Number the statements below 1, 2, and 3 to show the order in which the events took place.

_____ a. Hopscotch boxes were drawn on the ground.

_____ b. The player hopped from one box to another in number order.

_____ c. The player tossed the pebble into box 1.

4. Making Correct Inferences

Two of the statements below are correct *inferences,* or reasonable guesses. They are based on information in the passage. The other statement is an incorrect, or faulty, inference. Label the statements C for *correct* inference and F for *faulty* inference.

_____ a. Playing games helped children to develop their motor skills.

_____ b. Remembering and following the rules of a game helps children develop thinking skills.

_____ c. Children who perform well at children's games will become better citizens as adults.

5. Understanding Main Ideas

One of the statements below expresses the main idea of the passage. One statement is too general, or too broad. The other explains only part of the passage; it is too narrow. Label the statements M for *main idea*, B for *too broad*, and N for *too narrow*.

_____ a. Hopscotch was played with pebbles as markers.

_____ b. There is a lot to know about the Renaissance period.

_____ c. Renaissance children played some games that are still played today.

Correct Answers, Part A _____

Correct Answers, Part B _____

Total Correct Answers _____

Confederate Women Spies

Women served as spies during the American Civil War. This was especially true for the Confederate, or rebel, army. A network of women spies worked behind Union lines. They told the rebels about Union plans.

Belle Boyd is one of the most famous of these spies. Boyd began her spying career when she was 16 years old. Union troops were occupying her hometown in Virginia, and Boyd listened in on their conversations. Any useful information she heard she passed on to Confederate forces. Later Boyd acquired key information about Union troop movements. She gained the confidence of a Union soldier and picked his pocket to learn the secret sign she needed to pass through Union lines. Boyd gave this vital information to Stonewall Jackson. He used it to win five victories over Union troops.

After Boyd was arrested and jailed several times for spying, she limited her activities to carrying messages to Europe. Boyd was on board the Confederate ship *Greyhound* when it was captured by a Union ship. She charmed the Union captain. He was so taken with Boyd that he helped her to reach Canada. From there, she carried her Confederate messages to England. In 1864 Boyd and the captain were married.

Nancy Hart was another well-known spy. She grew up in West Virginia. Determined to aid the rebel cause, Hart began to trade with the Union army. She sold eggs and vegetables to the soldiers. While trading with them, she made notes on the strength of the troops. She wandered through the camps, attempting to overhear battle plans. Whatever she learned she passed on to the Confederate army. Hart knew the West Virginia landscape inside out. She acted as a guide for Stonewall Jackson and his men. She led the rebels through this wild country on unmapped paths to attack the Union troops.

Angered by Hart's spying, the Union offered a large reward for her capture. In July 1862, Hart was captured in Summersville, West Virginia. She was in her early twenties when she became a Union prisoner. Hart tried her best to charm the Union soldiers, and her charm worked. She actually talked her jailer into giving her his gun and then shot him with it! She then jumped out the window of the jail. She hopped onto a nearby horse and escaped. One week later, Hart led Confederate troops to Summersville. There they fought and captured some Union troops.

Reading Time _____

Recalling Facts

1. The women described in the passage spied on
   - ❏ a. Confederate troops.
   - ❏ b. Union troops.
   - ❏ c. Confederate and Union troops.

2. Stonewall Jackson used Belle Boyd's information to
   - ❏ a. win five battles against Union troops.
   - ❏ b. gain a reward for her capture.
   - ❏ c. capture a ship headed for Europe.

3. The Confederate ship *Greyhound* was
   - ❏ a. headed for Canada.
   - ❏ b. transporting Union troops south.
   - ❏ c. captured by Union troops.

4. Nancy Hart helped Stonewall Jackson by
   - ❏ a. guiding his troops on unmapped paths.
   - ❏ b. selling him eggs and vegetables.
   - ❏ c. telling him Confederate battle plans.

5. Hart got out of jail by
   - ❏ a. charming the ship's captain.
   - ❏ b. marrying the soldier who guarded her.
   - ❏ c. shooting her jailer after getting his gun.

Understanding Ideas

6. From the information in the passage, one can infer that the ship *Greyhound* was
   - ❏ a. heading for Union troops.
   - ❏ b. heading for Europe.
   - ❏ c. captained by Stonewall Jackson.

7. One can conclude that after leaving the Summersville jail, Hart
   - ❏ a. returned home to West Virginia.
   - ❏ b. told Confederate troops that some Union troops were in the town.
   - ❏ c. was later captured and tried for the murder of the jailer.

8. In contrast to the traditional view of women in the nineteenth century, the Confederate women spies were
   - ❏ a. well educated and used their formal learning against the enemy.
   - ❏ b. not afraid to put themselves in danger.
   - ❏ c. both well educated and not afraid to face dangerous situations.

9. Boyd and Hart were similar in that both
   - ❏ a. used charm to escape from capture.
   - ❏ b. carried messages to Europe.
   - ❏ c. were hanged for spying against the Union.

10. According to the passage, with which of the following statements about the women spies would the author agree?
    - ❏ a. The spies were nasty, vicious women.
    - ❏ b. The spies were resourceful.
    - ❏ c. The spies were young and naïve.

24 B   The Moon Sisters

Sisters Ginnie and Lottie Moon were Confederate spies during the Civil War. The sisters lived in Ohio, where Lottie met and married Jim Clark. When Ginnie left college, she lived with the couple. Members of a pro-South group met in the Clark house. Some had carried covert messages from the North to the South.

One day, Lottie offered to carry a message to Kentucky. She disguised herself as an old woman. She delivered the message without any trouble. Lottie was a gifted actress, who often applied her gifts when spying.

Meanwhile, Ginnie had moved to Memphis. She began carrying messages back and forth for the South, pretending that she was traveling to see her sweetheart.

By this time, the Union suspected that the Moon sisters were engaged in espionage. Once, Ginnie was on a train that was searched by Union soldiers. Ginnie pulled a gun on them. She told them that she was a Union general's friend. The soldiers believed her and left. Then Ginnie ate the paper containing the secret messages.

Eventually, Ginnie was arrested. Lottie, in disguise, came to see her. Lottie then was also arrested. However, both were eventually released. Lottie headed home to Ohio. Ginnie moved to Hollywood, where she played small roles in two 1920s silent movies.

1. **Recognizing Words in Context**

   Find the word *covert* in the passage. One definition below is closest to the meaning of that word. One definition has the opposite or nearly the opposite meaning. The remaining definition has a completely different meaning. Label the definitions C for *closest*, O for *opposite or nearly opposite*, and D for *different*.

   _____ a. intelligent

   _____ b. hidden

   _____ c. public

2. **Distinguishing Fact from Opinion**

   Two of the statements below present *facts*, which can be proved. The other statement is an *opinion*, which expresses someone's thoughts or beliefs. Label the statements F for *fact* and O for *opinion*.

   _____ a. Lottie married Jim Clark.

   _____ b. Ginnie pulled a gun on the soldiers in the train.

   _____ c. Lottie was a gifted actress.

3. **Keeping Events in Order**

Number the statements below 1, 2, and 3 to show the order in which the events took place.

_____ a. Ginnie pulled a gun on the soldiers.

_____ b. Ginnie ate the paper containing a secret message.

_____ c. Union soldiers searched the train.

4. **Making Correct Inferences**

Two of the statements below are correct *inferences,* or reasonable guesses. They are based on information in the passage. The other statement is an incorrect, or faulty, inference. Label the statements C for *correct* inference and F for *faulty* inference.

_____ a. Jim Clark supported the Confederacy.

_____ b. Soldiers were usually on the alert for women spies.

_____ c. Lottie and Ginnie loved risk and adventure.

5. **Understanding Main Ideas**

One of the statements below expresses the main idea of the passage. One statement is too general, or too broad. The other explains only part of the passage; it is too narrow. Label the statements M for *main idea,* B for *too broad,* and N for *too narrow.*

_____ a. Lottie's disguises helped her be a successful spy.

_____ b. Lottie and Ginnie Moon were clever spies for the Confederacy.

_____ c. The Union and the Confederacy successfully used women to spy.

Correct Answers, Part A _____

Correct Answers, Part B _____

Total Correct Answers _____

Early Days of the Grand Canal

China is a very big country. It is slightly bigger than the United States in land area. It is a country of many resources. Among its resources are many great rivers, which provide useful transport routes. Water transport is an efficient way to carry heavy loads, such as grain.

In ancient times, a waterway was needed between China's rich farmlands and the capital city. This need inspired engineers to build a canal. According to writings by the ancient thinker Confucius, work on a canal linking the Yangtze River with the city of Huai-yin began about 486 B.C. For many centuries afterward, Chinese emperors worked on extending this ancient canal.

This canal is now known as the Da Yun He—or, in English, China's Grand Canal. One thousand years after the original canal was begun, it was in extreme need of repair. This was in the year 607, during the Sui Dynasty. By 610 the emperor had had the canal extended. The Grand Canal formed a northeast-southwest link between Huang Ho in the north and the Huai River in the south. The canal remained the main waterway in this part of China for the next five hundred years.

In the thirteenth century, the Mongols had conquered China. The Yuan dynasty established Beijing as the capital. The city's growing population needed food, so a new canal was built to extend shipping. Building this part of the Grand Canal required enormous effort and cost. Neither the first attempt nor the second one was successful, so the builders chose another route. Finally this link in the Grand Canal was finished. However, merchants found that using it for shipping cost too much. Instead, they shipped food to Beijing via sea.

By the time of the Ming dynasty (1368–1644), the Grand Canal had six sections. These were busy with cargo until the nineteenth century. Then a series of severe floods struck China. Parts of the Grand Canal were badly damaged. By 1868 it had been largely abandoned as a means of water transport. In time it fell into serious disrepair, especially along its northern route.

The Grand Canal was mostly restored in the twentieth century. It was widened and deepened, and a new section was constructed. Today the canal, which is about 1,200 miles in length, has new locks. It is busy with ships and barges carrying goods to and from cities along its banks.

Reading Time _____

Recalling Facts

1. The earliest record of the building of the Grand Canal in China was recorded by Confucius, who was a
   - ❑ a. Chinese merchant.
   - ❑ b. Chinese thinker.
   - ❑ c. Buddhist priest.

2. The first large-scale restoration of the original canal occurred in about
   - ❑ a. 480 B.C.
   - ❑ b. A.D. 607.
   - ❑ c. A.D. 1126.

3. The Grand Canal connects regions of China by extending from
   - ❑ a. east to west.
   - ❑ b. north to west.
   - ❑ c. northeast to southwest.

4. The Grand Canal was first built in ancient times to provide
   - ❑ a. water transport between farmlands and the capital.
   - ❑ b. irrigation for farmlands.
   - ❑ c. efficient transportation for the emperor's army.

5. Today, the Grand Canal is approximately _____ miles long.
   - ❑ a. 100
   - ❑ b. 750
   - ❑ c. 1,200

Understanding Ideas

6. One can conclude from the passage that the Grand Canal was built to
   - ❑ a. connect some of China's rivers.
   - ❑ b. defend China against invading Mongols.
   - ❑ c. improve food production in agricultural regions of China.

7. In the twelfth century, compared with shipping costs on the Grand Canal, shipping food via sea routes was
   - ❑ a. much more expensive.
   - ❑ b. considerably less expensive.
   - ❑ c. about the same cost.

8. One can infer from the passage that a system of constructed waterways was desirable in China because it
   - ❑ a. is a very mountainous country.
   - ❑ b. has an enormous coastline.
   - ❑ c. has many easily navigable rivers.

9. From the passage, one can conclude that ancient engineers who began the Grand Canal
   - ❑ a. worked with limited knowledge and had crude skills.
   - ❑ b. found a brilliant and enduring solution to their transportation problem.
   - ❑ c. were awarded a great deal of money for their achievement.

10. Considering its history, one can predict that in the future the Grand Canal will probably
    - ❑ a. need to be repaired and rebuilt.
    - ❑ b. change from a shipping route to a recreation area.
    - ❑ c. be abandoned in favor of air freight.

25 | B | A Trip Down the Grand Canal

The Grand Canal tour begins at Nanjing, which was China's capital during the Ming dynasty in the 1400s. Here people can see Ming palaces and temples, which have colorful, painted walls and upturned eaves.

The tour boat continues down the canal. It passes the quaint city of Kangxi. It floats on, beneath ancient bridges, including the famous Five-Pavilion Bridge.

Next the boat heads east. It enters Lake Taihu, one of China's most beautiful lakes. From this tranquil setting, the tour moves on to the equally peaceful Xihui Park. The park contains a natural spring. Emperor Qianlong thought the spring very striking, so he re-created it in his Beijing Palace.

Suzhou is the chief port along the Grand Canal. In the city, rows of houses and small piers can be seen not far from a large port. In the 1300s, the city was China's silk-making center. Visitors can tour both old and modern museums. In one museum, one can see how silk is made and woven into cloth. One can also spend an afternoon in one of Suzhou's elaborate gardens.

As the Grand Canal tour ends, the boat travels to peaceful West Lake. Visitors can spend a few hours at the fragrant tea fields nearby. A visit to Solitary Hill—the retreat of Li Bai, one of China's greatest poets—completes the tour.

1. **Recognizing Words in Context**

   Find the word *tranquil* in the passage. One definition below is closest to the meaning of that word. One definition has the opposite or nearly the opposite meaning. The remaining definition has a completely different meaning. Label the definitions C for *closest*, O for *opposite or nearly opposite*, and D for *different*.

   _____ a. peaceful

   _____ b. loud

   _____ c. healthy

2. **Distinguishing Fact from Opinion**

   Two of the statements below present *facts*, which can be proved. The other statement is an *opinion*, which expresses someone's thoughts or beliefs. Label the statements F for *fact* and O for *opinion*.

   _____ a. Kangxi is on the Grand Canal.

   _____ b. The springs were beautiful.

   _____ c. Tea is grown near West Lake.

3. Keeping Events in Order

Number the statements below 1, 2, and 3 to show the order in which the events took place.

_____ a. The tour boat heads east and enters Lake Taihu.

_____ b. The tourists see palaces and temples in Nanjing.

_____ c. The tour visits Solitary Hill—the retreat of Li Bai, one of China's greatest poets.

4. Making Correct Inferences

Two of the statements below are correct *inferences,* or reasonable guesses. They are based on information in the passage. The other statement is an incorrect, or faulty, inference. Label the statements C for *correct* inference and F for *faulty* inference.

_____ a. Little can be seen from the tour boat of the Grand Canal.

_____ b. The Chinese maintain very old bridges.

_____ c. Suzhou is a center of Chinese commerce and trade.

5. Understanding Main Ideas

One of the statements below expresses the main idea of the passage. One statement is too general, or too broad. The other explains only part of the passage; it is too narrow. Label the statements M for *main idea,* B for *too broad,* and N for *too narrow.*

_____ a. A visit to Solitary Hill— the retreat of Li Bai, one of China's greatest poets— completes the Grand Canal tour.

_____ b. Many interesting and historical sites can be seen along the Grand Canal tour.

_____ c. Taking tours of waterways is a good way to see the sights.

Correct Answers, Part A _____

Correct Answers, Part B _____

Total Correct Answers _____

ANSWER KEY

READING RATE GRAPH

COMPREHENSION SCORE GRAPH

COMPREHENSION SKILLS PROFILE GRAPH

ANSWER KEY

1A	1. b	2. c	3. a	4. b	5. c	6. b	7. c	8. a	9. b	10. b
1B	1. O, C, D	2. F, O, F	3. 3, 1, 2	4. F, C, C	5. N, M, B					
2A	1. b	2. c	3. a	4. a	5. a	6. b	7. a	8. b	9. c	10. a
2B	1. D, C, O	2. O, F, F	3. 3, 1, 2	4. C, C, F	5. B, N, M					
3A	1. a	2. c	3. b	4. c	5. a	6. a	7. c	8. b	9. a	10. c
3B	1. O, C, D	2. F, O, F	3. 2, 1, 3	4. C, C, F	5. N, B, M					
4A	1. b	2. c	3. b	4. c	5. b	6. c	7. b	8. c	9. c	10. a
4B	1. O, D, C	2. F, O, F	3. 1, 3, 2	4. C, F, C	5. M, B, N					
5A	1. b	2. c	3. a	4. b	5. a	6. c	7. c	8. c	9. a	10. b
5B	1. O, C, D	2. F, F, O	3. 3, 1, 2	4. F, C, C	5. M, N, B					
6A	1. a	2. b	3. b	4. c	5. a	6. b	7. a	8. c	9. c	10. b
6B	1. C, O, D	2. O, F, F	3. S, A, S	4. C, F, C	5. N, M, B					
7A	1. c	2. b	3. a	4. b	5. c	6. b	7. c	8. a	9. b	10. c
7B	1. O, C, D	2. F, O, F	3. 1, 3, 2	4. F, C, C	5. B, M, N					
8A	1. c	2. a	3. c	4. b	5. a	6. b	7. a	8. b	9. c	10. a
8B	1. C, O, D	2. O, F, F	3. 2, 1, 3	4. C, C, F	5. N, B, M					
9A	1. a	2. c	3. b	4. c	5. b	6. b	7. a	8. c	9. a	10. b
9B	1. C, D, O	2. F, F, O	3. 2, 3, 1	4. F, C, C	5. B, M, N					
10A	1. b	2. c	3. b	4. c	5. b	6. c	7. b	8. c	9. c	10. a
10B	1. O, D, C	2. F, O, F	3. 1, 3, 2	4. C, F, C	5. M, N, B					
11A	1. b	2. b	3. b	4. c	5. a	6. c	7. b	8. a	9. c	10. a
11B	1. O, C, D	2. F, F, O	3. 1, 2, 3	4. F, C, C	5. N, M, B					
12A	1. b	2. c	3. a	4. b	5. b	6. c	7. a	8. c	9. a	10. b
12B	1. O, D, C	2. F, O, F	3. 1, 3, 2	4. C, C, F	5. M, N, B					
13A	1. c	2. a	3. b	4. b	5. c	6. a	7. c	8. b	9. b	10. a
13B	1. O, C, D	2. O, F, F	3. 2, 1, 3	4. C, F, C	5. N, B, M					

14A	1. a	2. a	3. b	4. c	5. a	6. b	7. c	8. a	9. b	10. a
14B	1. C, O, D	2. F, O, F	3. 3, 1, 2	4. C, C, F	5. M, N, B					
15A	1. b	2. c	3. a	4. a	5. b	6. a	7. b	8. c	9. c	10. c
15B	1. O, D, C	2. F, F, O	3. 1, 3, 2	4. F, C, C	5. M, B, N					
16A	1. c	2. a	3. a	4. b	5. c	6. a	7. b	8. c	9. c	10. a
16B	1. D, C, O	2. O, F, F	3. 3, 2, 1	4. C, F, C	5. N, B, M					
17A	1. a	2. c	3. b	4. c	5. b	6. a	7. c	8. a	9. b	10. b
17B	1. C, D, O	2. F, F, O	3. 3, 1, 2	4. C, C, F	5. N, M, B					
18A	1. a	2. a	3. c	4. b	5. b	6. a	7. c	8. c	9. a	10. c
18B	1. O, C, D	2. F, O, F	3. 2, 1, 3	4. C, F, C	5. N, B, M					
19A	1. c	2. b	3. a	4. b	5. a	6. b	7. c	8. a	9. c	10. b
19B	1. D, C, O	2. O, F, F	3. 3, 2, 1	4. F, C, C	5. M, N, B					
20A	1. b	2. a	3. c	4. c	5. c	6. b	7. c	8. c	9. a	10. c
20B	1. O, C, D	2. F, O, F	3. 2, 3, 1	4. C, C, F	5. N, M, B					
21A	1. a	2. c	3. b	4. c	5. b	6. b	7. a	8. a	9. c	10. b
21B	1. C, O, D	2. F, F, O	3. 3, 1, 2	4. C, F, C	5. M, N, B					
22A	1. a	2. b	3. c	4. a	5. b	6. c	7. b	8. c	9. a	10. b
22B	1. D, O, C	2. F, F, O	3. 2, 1, 3	4. F, C, C	5. B, M, N					
23A	1. b	2. c	3. a	4. c	5. a	6. b	7. b	8. a	9. c	10. b
23B	1. O, C, D	2. O, F, F	3. 1, 3, 2	4. C, C, F	5. N, B, M					
24A	1. b	2. a	3. c	4. a	5. c	6. b	7. b	8. b	9. a	10. b
24B	1. D, C, O	2. F, F, O	3. 2, 3, 1	4. C, F, C	5. N, M, B					
25A	1. b	2. b	3. c	4. a	5. c	6. a	7. b	8. c	9. b	10. a
25B	1. C, O, D	2. F, O, F	3. 2, 1, 3	4. F, C, C	5. N, M, B					

READING RATE

Put an X on the line above each lesson number to show your reading time and words-per-minute rate for that lesson.

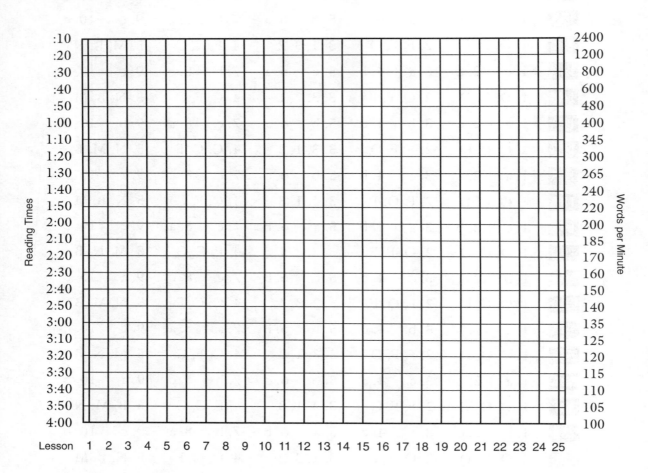

116

COMPREHENSION SCORE

Put an X on the line above each lesson number to indicate your total correct answers and comprehension score for that lesson.

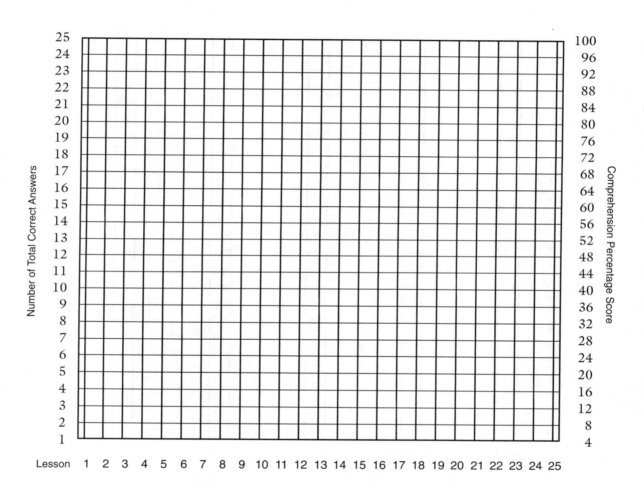

COMPREHENSION SKILLS PROFILE

Put an X in the box above each question type to indicate an incorrect reponse to any part of that question.

Lesson	Recognizing Words in Context	Distinguishing Fact from Opinion	Keeping Events in Order	Making Correct Inferences	Understanding Main Ideas
1					
2					
3					
4					
5					
6					
7					
8					
9					
10					
11					
12					
13					
14					
15					
16					
17					
18					
19					
20					
21					
22					
23					
24					
25					